MW01071169

WEAPON

THE PILUM

M.C. BISHOP

Series Editor Martin Pegler

First published in Great Britain in 2017 by Osprey Publishing,
PO Box 883, Oxford, OX1 9PL, UK
1385 Broadway, 5th Floor, New York, NY 10018, USA
E-mail: info@ospreypublishing.com

Osprey Publishing, part of Bloomsbury Publishing Plc

A CIP catalogue record for this book is available from the British
Library.

Print ISBN: 978 1 4728 1588 0
PDF e-book ISBN: 978 1 4728 1589 7
ePub e-book ISBN: 978 1 4728 1590 3
XML ISBN: 978 1 4728 2339 7

Index by Rob Munro
Typeset in Sabon and Univers
Originated by PDQ Media, Bungay, UK
Printed in China through World Print Ltd.

17 18 19 20 21   10 9 8 7 6 5 4 3 2 1

Osprey Publishing supports the Woodland Trust, the UK's
leading woodland conservation charity. Between 2014 and 2018
our donations are being spent on their Centenary Woods project
in the UK.

To find out more about our authors and books visit www.
ospreypublishing.com. Here you will find extracts, author
interviews, details of forthcoming events and the option to sign
up for our newsletter.

Acknowledgements

I am grateful to a number of individuals who have helped me in
preparing this volume. Sean Richards of re-enactment group
legio IX Hispana in California very kindly launched a *pilum* on its
longest journey ever (possibly) when he sent me a reconstruction
of one many years ago. To Sean, for that very generous act, I owe
a special debt of gratitude. Cometh the hour, cometh the *pilum*: it
now features in both photographs and tests within this book. I am
indebted to Barbara Birley and the Vindolanda Trust,
Jon Coulston, Evan Chapman (through the good offices of
Mark Lewis), Holger von Grawert, Fernando Quesada Sanz,
Albert Ribera Lacomba and SIAM Adjuntament de Valencia and
Robert Vermaat for allowing me to use their photographs.
Salvatore Ortisi helped with references while Sander van Dorst
was kind enough to allow me to quote from his translation of
Arrian's *Ektaxis kata Alanoon*. David Sim very kindly set up some
experiments – both measured drop and field tests – which were as
instructive as they were fun, as well as proving ever ready to
discuss technical aspects of the use and manufacture of the
weapon. Particular thanks are due to John Smith, who gamely
posed for photographs demonstrating the carriage of the *pilum* at
Hod Hill, appropriately enough. I must also thank Jeremy
Armstrong, Jon Coulston and David Sim for agreeing to read and
comment upon preliminary drafts of the text. While this book has
certainly benefited from all of these contributions, all faults,
errors and idiosyncrasies that remain are my sole responsibility.
If any book ever needed input from my friend, the late Peter
Connolly, then this is it; I can only hope his shade is not too
offended by the result, and might in some small way be appeased
if I dedicate this book to his memory.

Editor's note

Metric units of measurement are used in this book. The Roman
foot (*pes*), abbreviated as Rft here, was *c.*296mm. The Roman
inch (*uncia*), abbreviated as Rin, measured *c.*24mm. For ease of
comparison please refer to the following conversion table:

1m = 39.37in
1cm = 0.39in
1mm = 0.04in
1kg = 2.20lb
1g = 0.04oz

Cover illustrations are (top) © M.C. Bishop, and (bottom)
© Osprey Publishing.
Title-page photograph: A relief from Croy Hill on the Antonine
Wall showing three legionaries armed with *pila*. (Photo: M.C.
Bishop)

Artist's note

Readers may care to note that the original paintings from which
the battlescenes in this book were prepared are available for
private sale. All reproduction copyright whatsoever is retained by
the Publishers. All enquiries should be addressed to:

Peter Dennis, 'Fieldhead', The Park, Mansfield, Nottinghamshire
NG18 2AT, UK, or email magie.h@ntlworld.com

The Publishers regret that they can enter into no correspondence
upon this matter.

CONTENTS

INTRODUCTION

In 58 BC, Julius Caesar confronted a force comprising the entire tribe of Helvetii intent on migrating into Gaul. His troops attempted to stop them:

> The legionaries, from the upper ground, easily broke the mass-formation of the enemy by a volley of *pila*, and, when it was scattered, drew their swords and charged. The Gauls were greatly encumbered for the fight because several of their shields would be pierced and fastened together by a single *pilum*; and as the iron became bent, they could not pluck it forth, nor fight handily with the left arm encumbered. Therefore many of them preferred, after continued shaking of the arm, to cast off the shield and so to fight bare-bodied. (Caesar, *Gallic War* 1.25.2–4)

Those two observations by Caesar – that several enemy shields were pinned together and the shank of the *pilum* bent so it could not be withdrawn – have condemned the *pilum* to being the most misunderstood of all Roman weapons: a javelin designed to stick in an enemy's shield. It is not unreasonable, although by no means guaranteed, to suppose that Caesar was an eyewitness to these events and that his account is reliable. Yet the truth behind the function of the *pilum* nevertheless lies within that short passage: it was indeed designed to pierce a shield, but that was by no means the end of its mission. The long, thin shank was intended to allow the weapon to use its momentum to continue its course and ultimately wound or even kill the unfortunate warrior behind that pierced shield. If it subsequently bent under its own weight and could not be thrown back then that was certainly an advantage, but it was a useful by-product, not the *raison d'être* of the *pilum*. What had intrigued Caesar – who had presumably seen a lot of *pila* thrown during his military career – enough to cause him to comment was that the Gauls were so close together that their shields overlapped (hence they were fixed together by the *pila*, which could pass through two).

The *pilum* was the signature heavy javelin of the Roman legionary infantryman since before the Punic Wars under the Republic until well into the Imperial period. Like musket volleys immediately before more recent armies clashed on the battlefield, a volley of *pila* was designed to weaken the impact of an enemy attack by disorganizing their front ranks, allowing the legionaries to get to work at close quarters with the *gladius*. In common with earlier, javelin-equipped armies on the Italian peninsula, Roman legionaries originally carried two *pila*, which were part of the 'legionary package' of weapons, together with the short sword and shield, used in a carefully synchronized and choreographed sequence. The legionary would throw his *pilum* and – while it was probably still in flight – draw his sword ready for the next stage of the attack. The impact of the javelins would therefore rapidly be followed by contact between the two forces. Although its design made it very difficult for an enemy to reuse it quickly, once a battle was won and the damaged weapons retrieved, the *pilum* could nevertheless be returned to a serviceable state with the minimum of effort and expertise by a Roman legionary without necessarily needing the facilities of a forge.

The *pilum* underwent a series of developments during its period of use by the Roman Army and several distinct variants are apparent as well as two very different methods of hafting it. A number of different types of head were tried, and representational evidence indicates that weights were added to improve penetrative power and throwing straps employed to increase range, but the essential form of an iron (consisting of head, shank and tang or socket) on a wooden shaft remained unchanged. However, it is abundantly clear that, at any given period, there was no one type of *pilum* in use, but rather a range of forms which gradually evolved over time. Perhaps the most telling development of all – the volley itself – was a uniquely Roman contribution, since it relied on organizational skills and a level of training that were to be found in few other armies in the ancient world. The sources – both literary and representational – also emphasize the *pilum*'s versatility, making it clear that it was not just used as a javelin and that legionaries quite happily employed it as a thrusting spear when necessary, even being prepared to receive a cavalry charge with it.

The question of the origin of the *pilum* has occupied scholars since the 19th century and has not been helped by the fact that the Romans themselves seem to have forgotten (or, at best, become confused about) how they acquired this distinctive weapon. One thing is certain: like most of their military equipment, the Romans inherited the *pilum* from one (or more) of the peoples against whom they fought and then made it their own. What is furthermore apparent is the legacy of the weapon in the Late Roman and Early Medieval periods, when its descendants found favour with various armies. Finally, its iconic role as a 'traditional' Roman weapon achieved a degree of fame in Hollywood's movie depiction of Rome. Along with the short sword and curved body shield, for many people the *pilum* still epitomizes the Roman legionary. The combination of the three made Rome's heavy infantry a force to be reckoned with.

DEVELOPMENT
Adopt then adapt

ORIGINS

The Roman habit of adopting and adapting enemy weaponry was well known, but one detail puzzled modern scholars: which weapon served as a model for the first Roman *pilum*? This simple question led to a dispute between two of the great archaeologists of the early 20th century, the Frenchman Adolphe Reinach and the German Adolf Schulten. Writing in 1907, Reinach believed the *pilum* to have had a Samnite origin and suggested that it was adopted by the Romans shortly after the Samnite Wars in the second half of the 3rd century BC. In contrast, Schulten, writing in 1914, preferred an Iberian origin, and felt that it was adapted from (what the Romans called) the *solliferr(e)um* and adopted at the same time as the *gladius Hispaniensis*, towards the end of the 3rd century BC. It is worth pointing out that Schulten had conducted an important series of excavations on the Roman siege works around the hilltop town of Numantia in Spain, so his advocacy of an Iberian origin is scarcely surprising, given the nature of the material he found there. Unlike the *pilum*, the *soliferreum* (there is a variety of spellings) was wholly made of

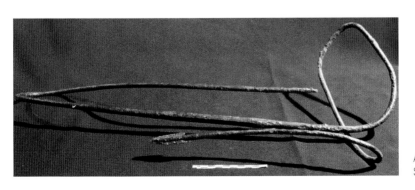

A *soliferreum* from Tózar-Moclin, Spain. (Photo: F. Quesada Sanz)

A Celtiberian *pilum/falarica* from Almedinilla, Spain. (Photo: F. Quesada Sanz)

0 ___ 2cm

iron (its name is a Roman joke: 'just iron'), so may seem unlikely as the direct ancestor of the *pilum*, although its influence may still have been relevant. The problem is that the classical sources disagree about the ultimate origin of the weapon. As Schulten pointed out, Livy (*History of Rome* 28.45.16) seems to have favoured the Etruscans, as did Pliny the Elder (*Natural History* 7.201), Plutarch (*Romulus* 21) and Propertius (*Elegies* 4.4.11) the Sabines, the so-called *Ineditum Vaticanum* the Samnites, and Athenaeus opted for the Iberians (*Deipnosophistae* 6.106F). What this confusion of opinions all too clearly indicates is that the Romans (and contemporary Greeks) did not know the true origin of the *pilum*.

The attraction of an Iberian prototype is obviously that it fits in with the adoption of the *gladius Hispaniensis* by the Roman Army, probably during the Second Punic War of 218–201 BC. The dagger (*pugio*) also seems to have had its origins in the region, so it is easy to see why it might be thought that the *pilum* shared these roots. However, it is clear that a *soliferreum* was not a *pilum*, but rather a *pilum*-like weapon. Literary descriptions of the *phalarica* (or *falarica*), another Iberian weapon, suggested it was a much closer match, with an iron attached to a wooden shaft. Schulten (1960: 1341) favoured its adoption after the Romans encountered Iberian troops fighting for the Carthaginians using such weapons in Sicily during the First Punic War of 264–241 BC, but it was a scholarly opinion, not backed up by incontrovertible evidence.

Various peoples around the Mediterranean used a javelin similar to what the Roman Army came to adopt during the 3rd century BC. The possibility that one or more types of javelin may have served as the prototype for the Roman weapon does not allow a clear resolution to the problem. However, it is worth reviewing the evidence to demonstrate the complexity of the questions involved.

Dionysius of Halicarnassus, writing in the 1st century BC, almost certainly anachronistically transferred the *pilum* of his own time back into the legendary period soon after Rome's foundation, when she was struggling against her Sabine neighbours:

> From the javelins (ὑσσός) that were fixed in the ground beside their tents (these javelins are Roman weapons which they hurl and having pointed iron heads, not less than three [Roman] feet [888mm] in length, projecting straight forward from one end, and with the iron they are as long as spears of moderate length) – from these javelins flames issued forth round the tips of the heads and the glare extended through the whole camp like that of torches and lasted a great part of the night. (Dionysius of Halicarnassus, *Roman Antiquities* 5.46.2)

Dionysius used the Greek word ὑσσός (which transliterates as *hyssos*) to indicate the *pilum*. The earliest mention we have of the *pilum* in Latin

('*Horatia pila*', Ennius, *Annals* 2.25) comes from the 3rd/2nd-century BC poet Ennius, marking the legendary defeat of the Curiatii by the Horatii in the 7th century BC.

A weapon resembling the *pilum* was certainly being used by Samnite warriors in the 6th and 5th centuries BC (Cowan 2012). Similarly, Gallic cemeteries in the north of Italy, such as that at Monte Bibele, have produced socketed *pilum*-like weapons with 500mm- to 950mm-long irons, with both leaf-shaped and barbed heads between 40mm and 170mm long, which dated to the 4th century BC (Lejars 2008). Similar weapons of the same date are known from the Celtic cemetery at Montefortino in Italy and (from the late 4th or early 3rd centuries) at La Tène in Switzerland. Etruscan evidence is also relevant here. A socketed *pilum* 1.2m long, from a grave at Vulci in Italy, has been variously dated to the 5th or 4th century BC and its form closely resembles the Gallic weapons just described. A decorated Etruscan copper-alloy vessel (*situla*) was found in Tomb 68 at Certosa, Italy. Generally held to date to the 6th century BC, the decoration on the vessel included warriors equipped with rectangular shields and pairs of spears, sometimes interpreted as *pila* (normally only one thrusting spear was carried, but two or more depicted suggests javelins for throwing). Additionally, a fresco in the 4th-century Giglioli Tomb at Tarquinia, Italy, depicts what have in the past been interpreted as *pila* alongside circular hoplite shields and a sheathed *xiphos*-type sword.

It was Livy who noted the similarity of the *pilum* to the *falarica*:

> There was used by the Saguntines a missile weapon, called *falarica*, with the shaft of fir, and round in other parts except towards the point, whence the iron projected: this part, which was square, as in the *pilum*, they bound around with tow, and besmeared with pitch. It had an iron head three [Roman] feet [888mm] in length, so that it could pierce through the body with the armour. But what caused the greatest fear was, that this weapon, even though it stuck in the shield and did not penetrate into the body, when it was discharged with the middle part on fire, and bore along a much greater flame, produced by the mere motion, obliged the armour to be thrown down, and exposed the soldier to succeeding blows. (Livy, *History of Rome* 21.8.10–12)

Livy was writing under Augustus, two centuries after the events he described, and his source for this statement is unknown. He may well have had access to a contemporary description of the Iberian weapon, or merely heard that it resembled the *pilum* and projected back his perception of a weapon with which he was familiar. On balance, the former is more likely than the latter, but caution in such matters is always advisable. Nevertheless, the key attributes of the *pilum* are matched by Livy's *falarica*: the long iron shank, its armour-piercing capabilities and its habit of encumbering an enemy shield (although here confused with its use as a fire weapon: Quesada Sanz 1997: 334–36). It is easy to see why Schulten, who had excavated *pila* in Spain, was convinced of an Iberian origin for the *pilum*.

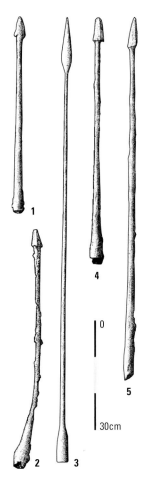

Prototype *pila* from Montefortino (**1**, **2**, **4**, **5**) and Vulci (**3**), 4th century BC. (Drawing: M.C. Bishop)

There is still no clear conclusion to the debate, even after so many years of new artefactual discoveries and a more nuanced approach to the study of the *pilum* and its ancestors. A broadly 'Celtic' origin seems likely (whether through Northern Italian or Iberian Celts, or even at one remove via another Italian culture such as the Etruscans or Samnites). In fact, any or even all of them are possible. Whether the two different methods of hafting the weapon – socketed and tanged – may have had different cultural origins is another matter altogether, and there does not as yet seem to be any way of proving this.

Ultimately, all that can be said is that a type of weapon closely resembling the *pilum* was common in the 4th century BC among peoples the Romans encountered and, by the end of the 3rd century BC, the Roman Army had adopted it as both their light and heavy legionary javelin. It therefore seems likely that the *pilum* was acquired at about the same time as the curved, oblong shield (nowadays generally referred to as the *scutum*, although the word could refer to any type of shield), but before the *gladius Hispaniensis*.

THE EVOLUTION OF THE *PILUM*

Mid-Republican

The Republican *pilum* described by Polybius existed in two basic forms – light and heavy – which in itself may be a clue to the fact that more than one weapon inspired the Roman javelin. The term *pilum* seems to have encompassed any javelin with a long iron attached to a wooden shaft. A javelin resembling a light form of the *pilum* was used by the *velites*, the skirmishing component of the mid-Republican Army and, as such, was a very different missile to its heavier cousin. Polybius' description is our main source and key to identifying archaeological examples of the weapon:

> The wooden shaft of the javelin measures about two cubits [*c.*924mm] in length and is about a finger's breadth [*c.*19mm] in thickness; its head is a span [*c.*231mm] long hammered out to such a fine edge that it is necessarily bent by the first impact, and the enemy is unable to return it. If this were not so, the missile would be available for both sides. (Polybius, *Histories* 6.22.4)

Livy calls this type of weapon the *hasta velitaris* (*History of Rome* 26.4.3), rather than a form of the *pilum*, but the description suggests otherwise. The length of the head or iron – like the shaft, two cubits – shows it to be related to both the light and heavy javelins carried by the main body of legionaries, a supposition that is also indicated by its non-returnability. Iron components answering to this description have been identified from Šmihel pod Nanosom (Slovenia), the camps around Numantia, and Caminreal (also in Spain). Peter Connolly reconstructed one which weighed just 0.23kg, including 0.09kg of iron components.

Polybius also describes both the light and heavy *pila* used by the *principes* and *hastati*, comprising the front and middle lines of a mid-Republican battlefield formation:

> The *pila* are of two sorts – stout and fine. Of the stout ones some are round and a palm's length [*c.*77mm] in diameter and others are a palm square. Fine *pila*, which they carry in addition to the stout ones, are like moderate-sized hunting-spears, the length of the haft in all cases being about three cubits [*c.*1.386m]. Each is fitted with a barbed iron head of the same length as the haft. This they attach so securely to the haft, carrying the attachment halfway up the latter and fixing it with numerous rivets, that in action the iron will break sooner than become detached, although its thickness at the bottom where it comes in contact with the wood is a finger's breadth and a half [*c.*29mm]; such great care do they take about attaching it firmly. (Polybius, *Histories* 6.23.9–11)

The earliest archaeological examples of what are almost certainly Roman heavy *pila* actually pre-date Polybius by some 50 years and are known from Talamonaccio in Italy (Luik 2000), the Spanish site of Castellruf (Álvarez Arza & Cubero Argente 1999) and Šmihel (Horvat 2002), all dating to the late 3rd or early 2nd century BC. Further examples of similar

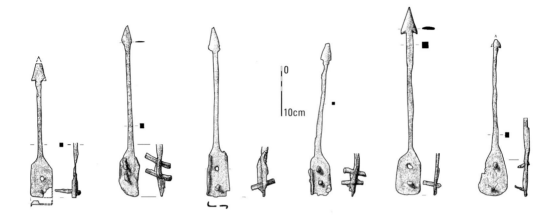

Telamon-type *pila* from Talamonaccio, late 3rd century BC. (Drawing: M.C. Bishop)

weapons are known from Ephyra in Greece (Luik 2000: 273–74), which probably date from the mid-2nd century BC (the Romans captured the site in 167 BC). Although these *pila* share a variety of characteristics and have been rather generally termed the Telamon type (named after the battle fought between the Gauls and Romans near the find site of Talamonaccio in 225 BC), there are subtle distinctions between some of the examples. The *pila* from Talamonaccio itself come in two forms: those with rectangular, flanged tangs and those with flat, rectangular (or sub-rectangular) tangs. All of the tangs were secured to the wooden expansions by means of two square-sectioned rivets and the flanges (turned up on one side and down on the other). With the complete ferrous component or iron (head, shank and tang) varying between 270mm and 325mm in length, the barbed heads (which were mostly lenticular in section) ranged between 34mm and 45mm. The tang plates varied between 75mm and 95mm in length and 40mm and 50mm in width. A small votive model of a *pilum* comes from the same site. Reconstructions by Peter Connolly suggest a weight of 0.265kg for the iron components and a total weight, once hafted, of 1.28kg.

The *pilum* irons from Castellruf were very similar to the first type of Telamon weapons, with the lobed tangs and barbed heads on short shanks. They varied between 378mm and 417mm in length, the lenticular-sectioned barbed heads between 32mm and 65mm. The tang plates were between 88mm and 109mm in length and 42mm and 52mm in width once folded.

The hoard from Šmihel was larger and more varied, including three distinct subtypes of tanged *pila* but also emphasizes the importance of the lighter, socketed *pila*, which are the predominant forms of the weapon in the hoard and may represent the light *pila* of the *velites*, *principes* and *hastati*. The Šmihel socketed *pila* were mostly headless or the shank was in fact one long, tapering, square-sectioned head. A variant of this 'headless' type included examples with O-shaped apertures, probably designed to contain flammable material in a similar manner to fire-arrows and fire-bolts. The sockets varied between 15mm and 21mm in diameter and the irons could be a total of 200mm to 380mm long. None of the socketed *pila* had barbed heads.

The second variety closely resembled the Talamonaccio and Castellruf *pila*, in that they had barbed heads, short shanks and large, lobed tangs secured with two rivets (occasionally one) which were folded over around the evidently rectangular expansions. Tang plates here varied between 66mm and 78mm in length and were generally 45mm in width, while irons could be 220mm to 298mm long, inclusive of tang and head. Peter Connolly's reconstruction of this type of *pilum* (2000: 45) weighed 1.38kg, of which 0.34kg was due to the ferrous components.

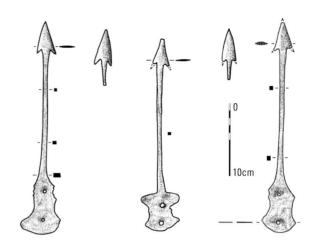

Telamon-type *pila* from Ephyra, mid-2nd century BC. (Drawing: M.C. Bishop)

The third type had the same lobed tang as the Telamon type but with longer and more slender shanks and smaller heads. These heads were usually lenticular, but in one case at least was quadrilobate. For these weapons, the tang plate was between 63mm and 81mm in length and between 37mm and 39mm in width, but irons could be a total of 321mm to 398mm long, including the tang and head. This type, when reconstructed, had ferrous components of 0.25kg and a total weight of 1.11kg.

A fourth variety had sub-rectangular tangs (with sloping shoulders) and two rivet holes in them but lacked the substantial lobes. In this case, the tang plate varied between 60mm and 81mm in length and 39mm and 48mm in width. Irons could be a total of 335mm to 570mm long, including the tang and head.

Many of the Šmihel *pila* show signs of bending, suggestive of damage during use, rather than any form of artefactual 'ritual killing' (which can be seen with some Spanish *soliferrea*). Most of these same types of damage will manifest themselves again in later *pila*.

It is noteworthy that most of the potential prototype *pila* from Spain and Northern Italy described above were socketed, and yet these earliest,

Telamon-type *pila* from Castellruf, late 3rd century BC. (Drawing: M.C. Bishop)

unequivocally Roman *pila* were mostly tanged. The tangs of the earlier examples were manufactured to be shaped like an hourglass, with 'wings' or lobes that were wrapped around either side of the wooden expansion of the shaft for a more secure means of attachment. With two iron rivets, there was quite clearly no intention for the tang to rotate within the expansion. Once the lobes were folded over, the tang was essentially rectangular and this in turn dictated the shape of the expansion of the wooden shaft. The

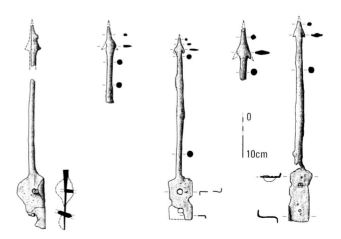

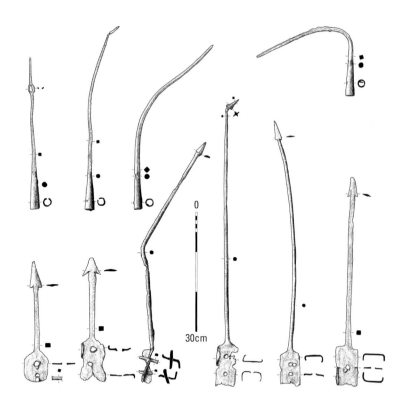

30cm

irons of these *pila* follow Polybius' description in having barbed heads and, as such, were intended to cause maximum damage to any individual unfortunate enough to be struck by one.

Another type of tanged heavy *pilum* was what might be called the Entremont type, named after an example found at a French hillfort site attacked by the Romans in the late 2nd century BC (Willaume 1987). Instead of the lobed, hourglass-shaped tang, this type tapered from a broad base, suggesting a conical expansion to the handle. Another example of this type of tang came from among the Talamonaccio finds, suggesting a degree of contemporaneity between the two types. The tang plate in this instance varied between 86mm and 126mm in length and 63mm and 69mm in width. Irons could be a total of 307mm to 321mm long, including the tang and head.

Two very different methods of hafting the *pilum* were used: the socket and the tang. These different techniques are found from the earliest through to the latest archaeological examples of the weapon, with no clear logic behind the differentiation. It may have been down to the preference of the manufacturer, the individual commissioning a batch, or there may even have been a tradition which has not survived as to which method should be used under any given circumstances. The tanged type certainly seems to dominate in the archaeological record, but it is difficult to judge

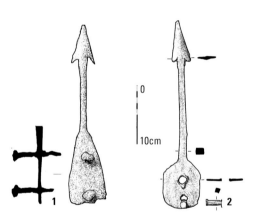

0

10cm

1

2

14

how far this reflects reality in antiquity. Indeed, it is conceivable that we are seeing a depositional bias caused by differing rates of attrition, perhaps because the tanged variety was more vulnerable to damage, rather than a true reflection of the popularity of the respective types. Tanged types were further subdivided between flat- and spike-tanged examples.

Late Republican

The Roman politician and general Gaius Marius (157–86 BC) has earned a place in the folklore of the *pilum* for an innovation attributed to him by Plutarch:

> It is said that it was in preparation for this battle that Marius introduced an innovation in the structure of the *pilum*. Up to this time, it seems, that part of the shaft which was let into the iron head was fastened there by two iron nails; but now, leaving one of these as it was, Marius removed the other, and put in its place a wooden pin that could easily be broken. His design was that the *pilum*, after striking the enemy's shield, should not stand straight out, but that the wooden peg should break, thus allowing the shaft to bend in the iron head and trail along the ground, being held fast by the twist at the point of the weapon. (Plutarch, *Marius* 25)

Although no example of a *pilum* has ever been found that could be interpreted as having employed one iron and one wooden rivet, it is difficult to dismiss this story without careful consideration (Matthew 2010). The problem with it is that archaeological examples of *pila* dating to both before and after Marius' supposed reform show that every care was taken to attach the tang to the shaft very securely. Comparison of excavated examples of pre-Marian *pila* with the examples from Oberaden, Germany (see p. 18) shows two main differences beyond a simpler and narrower tang. First, the later weapon now has a collet at the top of the expansion; second, there is an additional rivet through the tang, bringing the total to three. If anything, the tendency was to make the junction between the iron and shaft more, not less, secure. As Christopher Matthew observed, using a *pilum* with one wooden rivet in hand-to-hand combat was unthinkable. Moreover, the sort of rotation envisaged would not have been feasible without the tang being sufficiently free to move within its hafting and, inevitably, rattle around and possibly even work loose before it could even be used in battle (Grab 2011). Thus it looks as if this whole story might be a misunderstanding of a genuine reform of the weapon undertaken at some point and subsequently attributed to Marius. Ancient writers liked to identify prominent individuals as being responsible for innovations that may have had more humble origins. So what might the 'wooden rivet' really have been? There are a number of possible interpretations of the story beyond the oft-repeated and implausible literal one. A terminological misunderstanding on the part of Plutarch or his source, combined with the observed behaviour of the *pilum* in action, may have formed five by adding those two twos. Alternatively, the whole story

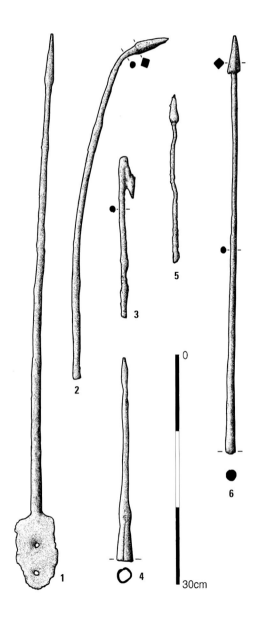

Renieblas-type *pila* from Numantia (**1**, **3**, **4**, **5**, **6**) and Cáceres el Viejo, Spain (**2**), mid-2nd century BC. (Drawing: M.C. Bishop)

OPPOSITE *Pila* from Caminreal, 1st century BC. (Drawing: M.C. Bishop)

may be a fabrication, designed to enhance Marius' reputation as a military reformer. It may even have originated as a joke within the Army (whose sense of humour was notoriously wry) and, in the manner of Chinese whispers, ended up being taken seriously by Plutarch. The wooden rivet of Marius therefore has to be treated with a healthy amount of scepticism until an archaeological example of its use can be proved (McDonnell-Staff 2011).

The heavier *pila* of the Late Republic developed longer, narrower shanks and smaller pyramidal heads and these are characterized by what Connolly termed the Renieblas type, named after the examples recovered from that and other Roman camps around Numantia and at Cáceres el Viejo (Spain). These still have fairly broad, flat tangs. Examples of a narrower-tanged type have been found at Valencia (Alapont Martin *et al.* 2010) and Caminreal (Vicente *et al.* 1997), both in Spain. At Caminreal, the rectangular tang was flanged on either side, recalling the lobes on earlier *pila*, designed to secure the tang within the expansion. The change from the large, barbed head to the much smaller pyramidal one suggests the nature of the target had changed and this may have been a response to the increasing occurrence of civil wars, with heavily armed and armoured legionaries pitted against each other. Pyramidal or bodkin heads were the best armour-piercing tips, designed to punch their way through a shield with the minimum resistance and then on through any armour protecting the target. Connolly's reconstruction of a Renieblas-type *pilum* weighed 1.71kg, 0.66kg being the weight of the ferrous elements.

Pila found at Caminreal and Osuna (Spain) probably belong to the civil war period, during the first half of the 1st century BC, while examples from Valencia are dated to the capture of that town by Pompey in 75 BC. Archaeological evidence reveals that one example was used to spit a prisoner after the capture of the town (Alapont Martin *et al.* 2010), just one of several atrocities recorded from the site. Lighter *pila* of the period again tended to be socketed, although spike-tanged examples are known.

As at Šmihel, some *pila* from this period have been recovered with no head and what appear to be sharpened tips to the shanks. Although some from Caminreal appear to have actually been made this way, it seems more likely that most were damaged, lost their heads and were then pressed back into service in that diminished state if still sufficiently sharp (see p. 43).

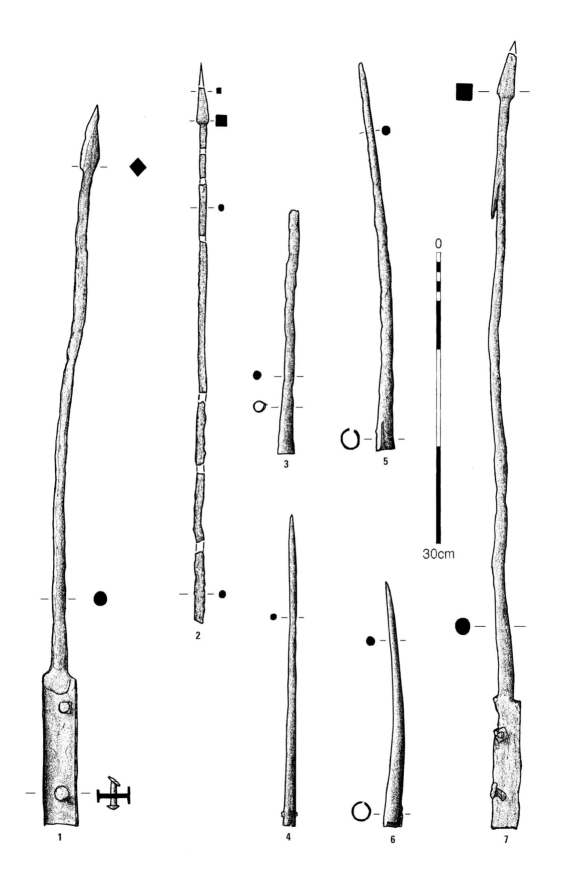

30cm

1

2

3

4

5

6

7

17

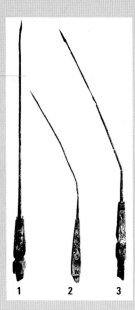

The three Oberaden *pila*. (From Albrecht 1942)

The Oberaden *pila*

The tanged *pila* found at Oberaden during the excavations by Christoph Albrecht in 1938 radically changed the way scholars looked at and reconstructed the weapon. They were at once such ordinary artefacts, but in a remarkable state of preservation (Albrecht 1942). Not only were the heads and shanks intact (although two of the three shanks were bent at more or less the same angle just above the expansion), but they were still hafted to the wooden shafts. They preserved some interesting details of *pilum* construction, such as the facts that the two rivets securing each tang to its shaft were each passed through square roves to help prevent them splitting the wood or that the collets were held in place with wedges.

The original published photographs (in a volume that is itself extremely hard to find, as only a few university libraries hold copies) show the original state just after excavation. Subsequent photographs show that there had been a marked deterioration in the organic components.

The other '*pila*' from Oberaden that have achieved a degree of fame were the so-called *pila muralia* (see p. 39). The Oberaden examples of these weapons were remarkable in that most bore inscriptions marking them as belonging to certain centurions.

More recent excavation at Oberaden has recovered further examples of the *pilum*, but none as well preserved as those first three.

Early Imperial

Archaeological examples of tanged *pila* are known from comparatively early in the Augustan period, excavated from Dangstetten (Germany) and dating to Drusus' Alpine campaign of 15 BC. These are the first examples of what is now known as the Oberaden type of *pilum*, named from well-preserved examples found at that fortress on the Lippe River in Germany from the later campaigns of Varus and his successor. With the iron varying between 765mm and 875mm and the heads between 40mm and 50mm in length, they are similar in size to Late Republican *pila*, which is scarcely surprising. In fact, contemporary sites along the Lippe, such as Haltern, have produced further examples of both tanged and socketed *pila* and their fittings, as has the site at Kalkriese, equated by many scholars with the site of the Varus disaster of AD 9. A *pilum* from Kalkriese (see p. 32), with a length of bent shank still attached, has a flange immediately below the pyramidal head, with the shank narrowed just above and below it, perhaps as an intentional point of weakness. A *pilum* tang and part of the wooden expansion also comes from Kalkriese and this has two cruciform-headed rivets (perhaps, like the roved Oberaden examples, to stop the wood splitting). *Pilum* heads, and less often the shanks, continue to be found on sites throughout the 1st century AD, a number coming from the Rhine River at Mainz (Germany). A well-preserved, 1.05m-long, corrosion-free example, complete with collet and part of the wooden shaft (formerly in the Guttmann Collection) appears to come from such a context. Two fine, round-sectioned shanks with their pyramidal heads still attached were excavated in the Roman fort within the hillfort at Hod Hill (England). Both were bent in the same place, indicating that they had seen action. Unfortunately, their method of hafting is missing but, from their lengths of 0.55m and 0.61m and the absence of any sign of broadening into a socket, they must have been tanged *pila*. Rectangular and trapezoidal tangs with two rivets are found, as are shorter rectangular tangs with a single rivet. It is difficult to see how such differences could be anything other than the result of the personal preferences of those manufacturing the weapons.

An important difference between Late Republican and Early Imperial *pila* was the adoption of the collet. Its introduction suggests that tanged *pila* were susceptible to splitting their wooden shafts. A hollow square in section, often tapering towards the top so that it appears pyramidal, the collet would have served to reinforce the top of the wooden expansion and thus help prevent it from splitting upon impact. Although collets are first found in the spike-tanged *pila* from Alesia (France), they were evidently thought suitable for use with the riveted tanged *pila* as well. The collets of the Oberaden *pila* are flat on top, as are examples from Haltern and Hod Hill (all the last decade of the 1st century BC), but slightly later (first decade of the 1st century AD) examples from Kalkriese have small projections at each corner on the top edge (and an example of this type was also found at Haltern). The tops of these projections clearly sat flush with the top of the expansion and did not protrude above it, since their interior faces match those of the rest of the collet below. All three of the Oberaden *pila* had their collets wedged in place, perhaps indicative of a design flaw. In fact, reconstruction *pila* will often shed their collets with use and the wedges were a simple solution to an evident (and reproducible) problem. A tanged *pilum* with a single rivet from more recent excavations than those that produced the famous three examples at Oberaden has a sophisticated integral collet that is reinforced with an external one driven down over the top of it. It is unclear whether this was intentional from the start or a field modification of a rather flawed attempt to solve the problem of splitting expansions.

Two bent *pilum* shanks, retaining their heads but lacking tangs, from Hod Hill. (© The Trustees of the British Museum. All rights reserved)

Socketed *pila*, both heavy and light, continue to be found from this period, but are inevitably overshadowed by the prominence given to tanged *pila* by the Oberaden finds. Even so, socketed *pila* come from Haltern, Oberaden and Windisch (Switzerland). The tradition of tanged heavy *pila* was clearly strong – at least 200 years old by the time the Oberaden *pila* were manufactured – but the occurrence of socketed heavy examples may be indicative of a gradual change taking place among some units, as this new form began to be adopted.

The most important change to the *pilum* seems to have been the addition of a weight attached to the shaft just below the expansion. This post-dates the adoption of the collet and is first seen on Frieze A of the Cancelleria reliefs, which features members of the Flavian Dynasty (AD 69–96), as well as praetorian guardsmen, and dates to the last quarter of the 1st century AD. Similar weights are also depicted on the Great Trajanic Frieze (reused on the Arch of Constantine in Rome) and on some of the metopes from the Tropaeum Traiani at Adamclisi (Romania). Both monuments date to the very beginning of the 2nd century AD. Weighted *pila* are also depicted on 2nd and 3rd-century military tombstones from Rome. Weights were almost certainly added to improve the penetrative capabilities of the weapon and the reason that this became necessary may

be that it was harder for the *pilum* to penetrate Roman plywood shields than the plank shields used by the traditional enemies of the Roman Army (see p. 24). In other words, the civil wars of the Late Republic and Early Empire drove the development of the weighted *pilum*.

Trajan's Column in Rome is of little help in discussing *pila* at the beginning of the 2nd century AD, and not just because it is an unreliable source for a number of reasons. In this instance, most Roman weapons were depicted with metal attachments, all of which have long ago vanished. At one point, in Scene V, some shafted weapons are visible in the background, but whether these are very thin spears or abnormally long *pilum* shanks is not clear.

Later Imperial

A light, socketed *pilum* was included within a hoard of weaponry and other material from Corbridge (England) and probably dated to the first half of the 2nd century AD. In fact, *pila* have been found at a number of 2nd-century AD sites, including those associated with both the Antonine Wall in Scotland and the Marcomannic Wars (AD 166–80) of Marcus Aurelius on the Danube River.

A group of 30 *pilum* heads from both the well in the headquarters building and the east gate at Bar Hill fort, on the Antonine Wall, are of interest, since they all appear to have fractured just below the head. Some have turned-over tips, suggesting they struck a hard surface when thrown. They may well have broken off after impact and those from the well may conceivably have been awaiting fire-welding back onto a shank (see p. 44). They are also depicted on a relief from Croy Hill, also on the Antonine Wall, showing one bearded and two unbearded legionaries, together with the usual curved, rectangular shields. Despite some weathering to the stone, the heads of two of the three *pila* can clearly be

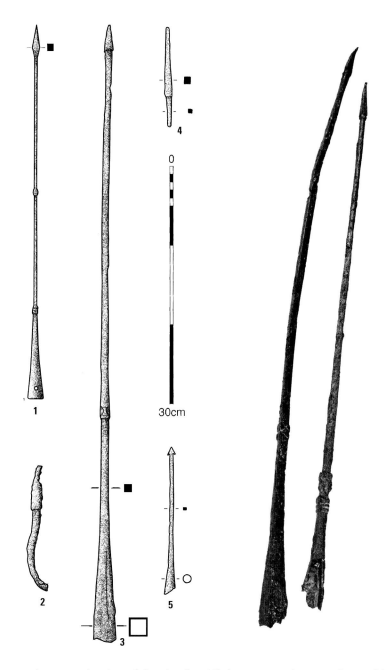

FAR LEFT Antonine *pila* from Eining-Unterfeld (**1**), Bar Hill (**2**), Lobith (**3**) and Iža, Slovakia (**4**, **5**). (Drawing: M.C. Bishop)

LEFT *Pila* from the 3rd-century AD battle site at Harzhorn. (Photo: Braunschweigisches Landesmuseum, I. Simon)

0

30cm

made out at the tips of the shanks. All three expansions survive and it is readily apparent there are no weights on these weapons. This relief can probably be dated to between *c*.AD 140 and 165.

Sites on or near the Danube associated with the Marcomannic Wars have produced socketed heavy *pila* from the vexillation fortress at Eining-Unterfeld, Germany, with small barbs. Other examples are known from Mušov-Burgstall (Austria) and Markt Berolzheim (Germany).

Finds from the 3rd century AD include *pilum* heads among a hoard of weaponry from a rampart-back store building in the legionary fortress at Caerleon (Wales). These have much longer heads than was standard

The *amentum*

A relief from Mainz depicts the 1st-century AD legionary P. Flavoleius Cordus of *legio XIIII Gemina* holding what is almost certainly a *pilum* (although the upper part of the weapon is damaged). His hand is depicted with forefinger and second finger resting in a throwing-strap or *amentum*, a simple aid designed to increase the range (or momentum) of a javelin. For this reason it is almost certainly a *pilum*, rather than a standard spear, that was originally depicted. The ancient sources make no mention of the use of a throwing strap in connection with the *pilum*, so this ambiguous representation is the only direct evidence. However, the tradition of using a throwing strap to assist with casting a javelin was common and can be seen, for example, on vase paintings in the 4th century BC.

RIGHT Detail of the tombstone of P. Flavoleius Cordus showing him holding an *amentum* or throwing strap. (Photo: M.C. Bishop)

in earlier periods, presumably to aid with balance and penetrative capability (by increasing mass). A single socketed shank 300mm long came from the area, dating to the same period, and that had lost its head. Similar long *pilum* heads have come from a workshop deposit in the western military compound at Corbridge, just south of Hadrian's Wall. As at Caerleon, this part of the military base can be associated with *legio II Augusta*, so it is no surprise that the two deposits appear to be contemporary.

More recently, the identification of a 3rd-century battlefield site at Harzhorn (Germany) has included socketed *pilum* finds, including two bent shanks with their heads and sockets intact, as well as heads with small barbs. These have been suggested as dating to a campaign by Maximinus Thrax against the Germans in the AD 230s. Interestingly, two of the *pila* have square sockets, suggesting that they were originally fitted to wooden shaft expansions. A similar square socket is present on a *pilum* from Lobith in the Netherlands. It is even possible that the Croy Hill legionaries could have had socketed *pila* with expansions, rather than tanged as might perhaps be expected. The sculpture is not detailed enough for any certainty. Nevertheless, the absence of tanged *pila* from the Later Empire would seem to indicate that socketed *pila* may have become the preferred form, both for light and heavy weapons, as early as the middle of the 2nd century AD.

These later *pila* often feature one or more small expansions or collars worked into the shank during forging. Rather than just an unnecessary piece of ornamentation, these details may represent the point of attachment for additional weights designed to increase the mass of the weapon even further and improve its penetrative capabilities when thrown. Although Early Imperial *pila* only seem to have had a single weight on the shaft, tombstones of the praetorian and urban cohorts indicate that more were added later.

PILUM DIMENSIONS FROM SOURCE TEXTS

Source	Item	Total length	Shaft length	Iron length	Head length	Date described	Date written
Dionysius of Halicarnassus (5.46.2)	*pilum*	–	–	888mm	–	5th century BC	1st century BC
Polybius (6.22.4)	*veles* javelin	1,155mm	924mm	231mm	–	2nd century BC	2nd century BC
Polybius (6.23.9–11)	heavy *pilum*	2,772mm	1,386mm	1,386mm	–	2nd century BC	2nd century BC
Polybius (6.23.9–11)	light *pilum*	2,772mm	1,386mm	1,386mm	–	2nd century BC	2nd century BC
Livy	*falarica*	–	–	888mm	–	late 3rd century BC	1st century BC
Vegetius (1.20)	*pilum*	–	–	216–296mm	–	pre-4th century AD	4th century AD
Vegetius (2.15)	*pilum* (*spiculum*)	1,844mm	1,628mm	216mm	–	pre-4th century AD	4th century AD
Vegetius (2.15)	*pilum* (*verutum*)	1,159mm	1,036mm	123mm	–	pre-4th century AD	4th century AD

DIMENSIONS OF EXCAVATED EXAMPLES OF PILA

Site	Iron length	Head length	Head width	Socket/tang	Date
Heavy prototype					
Vulci (Italy)	1,225mm	150mm	32mm	socket	5th/4th century BC
Light prototype					
Montefortino (Italy)	545mm	60mm	33mm	socket	4th century BC
Montefortino (Italy)	670mm	47mm	20mm	socket	4th century BC
Mid-Republican					
Talamonaccio (Italy), type 1	320mm	45mm	20mm	flat tang	late 3rd century BC
Talamonaccio (Italy), type 2	345mm	50mm	32mm	flat tang	late 3rd century BC
Šmihel (Slovenia)	269mm	45mm	30mm	flat tang	late 3rd/early 2nd century BC
Šmihel (Slovenia)	396mm	38mm	22mm	flat tang	late 3rd/early 2nd century BC
Ephyra (Greece)	326mm	44mm	31mm	flat tang	mid-2nd century BC
Ephyra (Greece)	331mm	49mm	32mm	flat tang	mid-2nd century BC
Castellruf (Spain)	382mm	>32mm	26mm	flat tang	late 3rd/early 2nd century BC
Castellruf (Spain)	420mm	>32mm	28mm	flat tang	late 3rd/early 2nd century BC
Late Republican					
Renieblas (Spain)	728mm	60mm	12mm	flat tang	2nd century BC
Caminreal (Spain)	745mm	67mm	16mm	flat tang	1st century BC
Early Imperial					
Oberaden E1 (Germany)	765mm	50mm	10mm	flat tang	early 1st century AD
Oberaden E3 (Germany)	875mm	40mm	7mm	flat tang	early 1st century AD
Unprovenanced	1,110mm	85mm	12mm	riveted spike tang	?1st century AD
Hod Hill 1 (England)	568mm	44mm	10mm	tanged?	mid-1st century AD
Hod Hill 2 (England)	507mm	43mm	10mm	tanged?	mid-1st century AD
Later Imperial					
Eining-Unterfeld (Germany)	780mm	32mm	12mm	socketed	mid-2nd century AD
Saalburg (Germany)	725mm	46mm	8mm	socketed	mid-3rd century AD
Angon					
Le Doubs à Pontoux (France)	930mm	56mm	14mm	socketed	early 6th century AD

FUNCTION AND DESIGN

The heavy *pilum* was clearly designed as a shock weapon. Its weight meant it was unsuitable for skirmishing, but it was also its chief strength at short range. Indeed, Livy wrote of 'the Roman *pilum*, which strikes, on being thrown, with a much harder impact than the *hasta*' (*History of Rome* 9.19.4). In its most refined form, the *pilum*'s energy at a comparatively short range, combined with the shape of its head, gave it the penetrative capability to pierce a plank shield (the type of layered plywood used on Roman shields is more resistant). The long iron shank then enabled it to continue in its trajectory into the body of the warrior wielding that shield. It was even capable of penetrating armour (Suda, s.v. *byssos*) or a helmet ([Caesar], *African War* 78.10). As Vegetius noted of the legion, 'it is equipped with javelins which no body armour nor shield are able to withstand' (*De Re Militari* 2.25.1, trans. the author).

Experiments undertaken by Reinach (1877–1917: 484) showed that his reconstructed *pila* could penetrate 15mm of oak or 30mm of fir when thrown from a distance of about 10m, matched by tests undertaken by Junkelmann (1986: 188–89), which pierced 20mm of plywood or 30mm of pine from a distance of 5m. More recent experiments by David Sim and the author confirmed that Roman plywood shields made of three layers of wooden strips laid crosswise were far more resilient to penetration by the *pilum* than plank shields – resilient but by no means impervious. Of course, much depends upon the accuracy of the reconstructions (particularly the shafts, of which so few survive), but such experiments serve to give a reasonable general impression of the likely capabilities of *pila*.

While this may be true of *pila* with an armour-piercing, pyramidal head, the heavy weapons of the Telamon and Entremont types with large, barbed heads were undoubtedly intended for use against unprotected flesh. As such, these were more obviously effective against unshielded opponents, or even cavalry, the size of the head being better suited to felling a horse than the bodkin head.

It is often said that the *pilum* shank was of soft iron and the head of steel, and the limited analyses that have been undertaken (Kmetič *et al.* 2004) can be interpreted as confirming this. Nevertheless, far too little

The anatomy of a *pilum* (opposite)

The classic Oberaden-type tanged *pilum*. The principal components of every *pilum* were an iron (**1**) attached to a wooden shaft (**2**, **3**). The iron comprised a head (**1a**), a long narrow neck or shank (**1b**) of round or square section (sometimes even both, one blending into the other) and a means of attachment to the shaft, so either a tang (**1c**) or a socket. The method of attaching the iron to the shaft used rivets (**3a**) that passed through both the wooden expansion on the shaft (**2a**) and the tang. Each rivet – the Oberaden *pila* had either two or three – was secured by peening or hammering it over a square washer or rove (**3b**). The assembly was made even more secure by the addition of a hollow, square ferrule, known as a collet (**3c**). The conical butt spike (**4**) was fitted to the bottom of the shaft and secured with a single nail (**4a**).

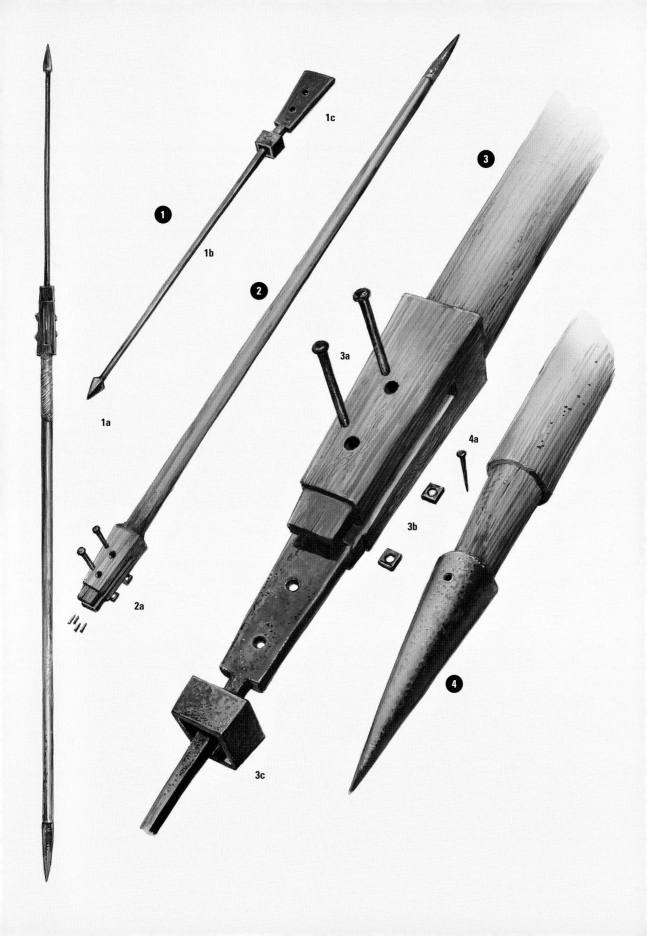

1

1a

1b

1c

2

2a

3

3a

3b

3c

4

4a

scientific examination has been undertaken for any certainty. Moreover, the only source to suggest this is Appian, describing (probably anachronistically) the Roman use of the *pilum* against the Gallic Boii in 358 BC: 'The spears of the Gauls were not like javelins, but what the Romans called *pila*, four-sided, part wood and part iron, and not hard except at the pointed end' (*Gallic Wars* 2.11).

Indeed, experiment shows that an iron head has exactly the same penetrative capabilities as a steel one so far as wood is concerned, but has the advantage of being easier (and quicker) to manufacture and easier to repair in the field if needed. Although early Roman *pilum* heads were barbed and lenticular in section, these were by and large replaced by small, pyramidal heads, square in section and often with small, residual barbs. Leaf-shaped heads are occasionally found on *pila* from all periods, recalling the Etruscan example from Vulci, but they were comparatively rare, as were single-barbed *pilum* heads like those from Osuna (Spain) and Filzbach-Voremwald (Switzerland).

Tanged *pila* could either be of a simple, spiked form, or a more complex flat design. Spike-tanged *pila* could be riveted and are known from Alesia, Oberaden and Haltern, but are far less common than the flat form. Flat, riveted tangs took the form of a rectangular extension of the shank with usually two holes for rivets and in the Republican period was lobed or flanged. This tang would then be fitted into a slot in the top of the wooden shaft, the rivets passed through square roves, and secured.

The wooden shaft had to be shaped for flat-tanged *pila* and so simple, coppiced poles without modification could not be used. The expansion was slotted at the top and drilled for rivet holes. In the Imperial period, in order to secure the entire assembly, an iron collet (a rectangular ferrule) was placed over the top of the expansion. On the Oberaden *pila*, this was held in place with wedges driven into the wood, once the tang had been riveted within the wooden expansion. Collets were slightly pyramidal, reflecting the taper of the expansion they topped. No such expansion was necessary with socketed *pila* and the lower end of the *pilum* iron with its socket could simply be nailed in place on the shaft, as can be seen on examples from Waddon Hill (England) and Eining-Unterfeld. Below the expansion, the surviving wooden shafts from the early 1st-century AD base of Oberaden had a diameter of between 23mm and 26mm (the modern Olympic specification for javelin diameter is 25–30mm).

A hand grip was added to the shaft at the point of balance by means of what was probably fine cord wrapped around the pole and glued in place. This is depicted on sculptural reliefs, such as Cancelleria Relief A from Rome, but did not survive (or, more likely, had never been applied) on the Oberaden *pila*. Other types of Roman spears and javelins do not seem to have had similar hand grips.

Cancelleria Relief A also confirms that the shaft was finished off with a conical iron shoe or butt, again nailed to the shaft. This allowed the *pilum* to be thrust into the ground – attested by Dionysius of Halicarnassus (*Roman Antiquities* 5.46.2) and Plutarch (*Sulla* 28.6) – and could also form a handy secondary weapon in close combat if the wooden shaft broke (as Polybius noted when discussing the cavalry spear: *Histories* 6.25.2).

Because *pilum* shafts tended to be of only slightly greater diameter than most spear shafts, it is difficult to distinguish *pilum* butts in the archaeological record from those of thrusting spears (*hastae*). Most excavations that have produced examples of *pilum* irons have produced conical ferrules that might have been attached to butts; the problem lies in proving a direct association.

One final component can be seen on sculptural reliefs, although no example has ever been found: an additional weight attached to the shaft. It is most clearly depicted on Cancelleria Relief A and the Great Trajanic Frieze. A spherical object, long presumed by scholars to be a weight, is attached below the expansion and above the hand grip – in other words, close to the centre of gravity. Similar weights are shown elsewhere on sculpture from this period and later.

Tombstone of M. Aurelius Lucianus of the Praetorian Guard in the Capitoline Museums, Rome, showing a *pilum* with two spherical weights and a wrapped or striped shaft. (Photo: M.C. Bishop)

PILUM MANUFACTURE

Although most spears and javelins could be hafted using poles cut from coppiced woodland with little modification, *pila* – especially the tanged variety with an expansion at the top – would have to be trimmed down from larger pieces of wood, probably being turned on a lathe. In order to obtain the greater diameter necessary to allow for the expansion, the shafts would have to have been cut from older, more developed poles, indicative of a need for careful woodland management. Although the type of wood used on the Oberaden *pila* was not examined before they were destroyed in World War II, ash was the most common wood used for spear shafts, with hazel as a second choice (presumably dependent upon available resources). A fragment of shaft still attached to an example of a tanged *pilum* from the Saône River at Saint-Germain-du-Plain (France) was made of ash (Feugère 1990).

Balance was key to the primary function of the *pilum* as a javelin. The early large barbed heads meant that the shank on a tanged *pilum* could only be fairly short, otherwise the wooden shaft would have to be extended (or fitted with a counterweight) to maintain the centre of gravity just below the expansion. Once the smaller, pyramidal head was adopted, the shank could be longer without affecting the balance due to the gearing effect. Making the tang smaller (as happened in the Late Republic) would also have enabled a smaller change, since it was closer to the centre of gravity and in part offset by the addition of the collet at the top of the shaft. When weights were first added, they were placed as close as possible to the point of balance, immediately below the expansion. All of this meant that careful attention had to be paid to the size and weight of the wooden shaft to ensure that it remained in harmony with the iron components and was not nose- or tail-heavy.

It has long been supposed that the *pilum* had a hardened steel tip and softer iron shank, and this does indeed seem to be true of Republican-period weapons (Kmetič *et al.* 2004). However, there is no evidence that this was the case for later *pila* like those from Oberaden (largely because the analysis has not been undertaken). Experiment using tools and methods appropriate for the period has shown that a tanged iron shank and head could be produced at the forge from an iron billet by a skilled smith and a semi-skilled striker in around 10½ hours, including finishing (Sim 1992). Producing a steel head would have taken considerably longer and, as experiment has shown (see p. 26), would have been an unnecessary elaboration. In all, the operation to make that one *pilum* consumed 13.5kg of charcoal and resulted in a 20 per cent loss of the original iron billet, despite minimizing the amount of filing needed through careful forging. This can be compared with similar experimental results, which showed that a simple javelin head (Sim's flat-bladed bolt head) could be made in just over half an hour, while a bodkin-headed catapult bolt (with similar armour-piercing qualities to the *pilum*, but a longer range) took less than one hour.

It is clear from this that the *pila* of a legion of around 5,000 men represented a considerable investment in resources (both materials and man-hours): some 67.5 tonnes of charcoal, 4.4 tonnes of iron (worked down to 3.5 tonnes), 50,000 man-hours of a smith's (and a striker's) time, as well as 5,000 coppiced poles, all assuming just one *pilum* per man. Of course, these would not all be produced at one time, but it does highlight how important retrieving *pila* after battle would have been for the Army.

As both Vegetius (*De Re Militari* 2.11) and the *Digest* (50.6.7, citing Tarrutienus Paternus) noted, each legion had within it both the facilities and the skilled staff to accomplish this during the Imperial period. It was a simple matter to produce the butt ferrule, while experiment has shown that a lead weight could have been slid onto the shaft and wedged in place or even cast directly onto the shaft, as may have been done with *plumbatae* (David Sim, pers. comm.).

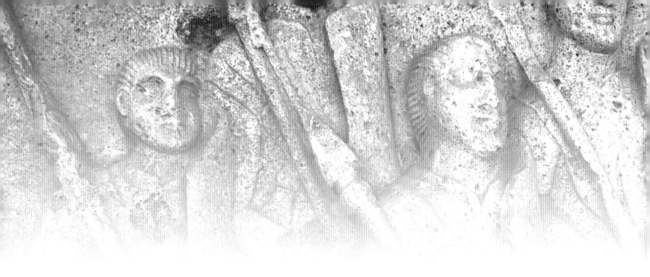

USE
The point of no return

SOURCES AND EVIDENCE

The Republican-period *pilum*

Knowledge of the use of the *pilum* in the earliest phase of its use by the Roman Army is non-existent. The literary sources are demonstrably unreliable; dealing with a period that was effectively prehistoric to them, they simply resorted to supplying detail from their own contemporary understanding of the *pilum*. Only general conclusions may be drawn, based on what we know of its use in later periods. Unfortunately, archaeology is not of much assistance until the time of our first reliable written evidence referring to the 3rd century BC, about which Polybius was writing.

Excavations in the 19th and early 20th centuries provided actual examples of *pila* from two separate sites. First came the work around Alesia sponsored by Emperor Napoléon III and undertaken by Eugène Stoffel from 1861 to 1865. This was followed by Adolf Schulten's excavations around Numantia in Spain in 1905–12. Although Alesia was a single instance of siege, the Spanish sites were clearly multi-period and more complex. Reconciling the archaeological and literary evidence was never going to be easy and even now remains open to reinterpretation, but this initial work provided a basis from which to begin the study of the *pilum*.

The oft-quoted opinion that the *pilum* was a weapon which supposedly could not to be returned once thrown is given the lie by Caesar himself, who tells (*Gallic War* 2.27) how the Belgae caught *pila* in mid-air and returned them against his men: no mean feat! This, however, was clearly exceptional and the incident serves to highlight one aspect of Caesar's writings, insofar as he was more likely to comment upon the unusual than

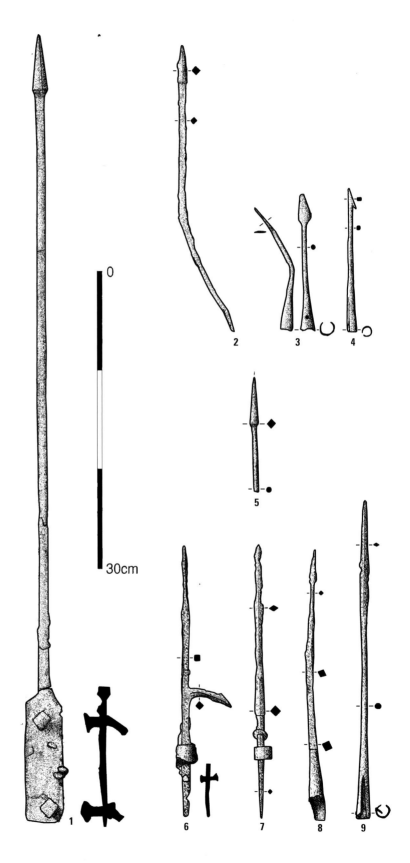

Pila from Valencia (**1**), Osuna (**2**, **3**, **4**, **5**) and Alesia (**6**, **7**, **8**, **9**), 1st century BC. (Drawing: M.C. Bishop)

0

30cm

the commonplace. Nevertheless, picking up expended *pila* did occur, and it is described by Livy in the context of the battle of Sentinum in 295 BC:

> The Gauls were standing in close order covered by their shields, and a hand-to-hand fight seemed no easy matter, but the staff officers gave orders for the *pila* which were lying on the ground between the two armies to be gathered up and hurled at the enemy's shield wall. Although most of them stuck in their shields and only a few penetrated their bodies, the closely massed ranks went down, most of them falling without having received a wound. (Livy, *History of Rome* 10.29.6–7)

This occurred during the Third Samnite War (298–290 BC), well before the usually accepted date for the adoption of the *pilum* by the Romans. Does this mean the account is untrustworthy? Livy may well have used a source which said the javelins were recovered in this way and inserted *pila* because those were what were familiar to him. On the other hand, if the *pilum* was indeed adopted by the Romans in the 4th century BC, then it becomes at least plausible. It is difficult to be certain and again demonstrates the caution with which written texts must be used. Livy (*History of Rome* 22.38.4) also mentions troops being allowed to leave their ranks to pick up discarded weapons at the battle of Cannae in 216 BC. Silius Italicus includes a vignette in his epic poem, the *Punica*, where Hannibal kills a young Roman, L. Manlius Volso, with a *pilum* he picked up from a pile of corpses, 'piercing his nostrils through his shield' (*Punica* 10.142–44).

The fact that *pila* could fall short is also mentioned in Livy's account of the defeat of the Gauls by a Roman army under M. Popilius Laenas and L. Cornelius Scipio in 350 BC:

> Their steady courage was aided by the fact that they were on higher ground, for the *pila* and *hastae* were not thrown ineffectively as often happens on level ground, but being carried forward by their weight they reached their mark. The Gauls were borne down by the weight of the missiles which either pierced their bodies or stuck in their shields, making them extremely heavy to carry. (Livy, *History of Rome* 7.23.8–9)

Scepticism over whether this is a genuinely contemporaneous account of the way in which *pila* were used is certainly justified, but it is an observation that Livy could well have drawn from his own time or more recent history (Zhmodikov 2000).

The Early Imperial *pilum*

For the first half of the 1st century AD, the spectre of civil war receded and Roman armies returned to fighting enemies that were generally organizationally inferior to them. In the context of Ostorius Scapula's campaign against Caratacus in Britain, Tacitus characterized the two types of troops used by Rome: 'If they offered a resistance to the

A *pilum* head from Kalkriese. (Photo: akg-images Museum Kalkriese)

auxiliaries, they were struck down by the *gladii* and *pila* of the legionaries; if they faced against the legionaries, they fell under the *spathae* and *hastae* of the auxiliaries' (*Annals* 12.35). Inevitably, civil war returned with the end of the Julio-Claudian dynasty in AD 68 and *pila* were once again needed to penetrate Roman shields. Perhaps tellingly, no missiles were exchanged during the fighting between Vitellian and Othonian forces at the battle of Bedriacum in AD 69, if Tacitus is to be believed. On the raised road that featured in the battle 'they struggled at close quarters, pressing with the weight of their bodies behind their shields; they threw no *pila*, but crashed swords and axes through helmets and breastplates' (Tacitus, *Histories* 2.42). During the Batavian siege of Vetera in AD 69–70, the Roman legionary defenders fought off those trying to scale the walls with the bosses of their shields and followed up with *pila* (Tacitus, *Histories* 4.29).

Two collets from Kalkriese. (Photo: akg-images Museum Kalkriese)

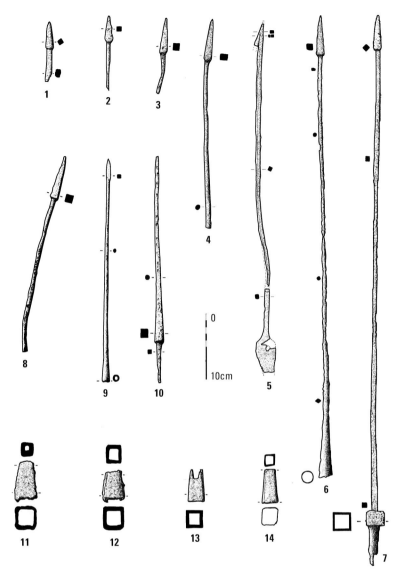

Early Imperial *pilum* components, including heads from Longthorpe, England (**1**) and Oberstimm, Germany (**2**, **3**); shanks from Windisch (**4**, **6**), Filzbach-Vordemwald in Switzerland (**5**), Saint-Germain-du-Plain (**7**), Dangstetten (**8**), Waddon Hill (**9**) and Rottweil, Germany (**10**); collets from Hod Hill (**11**, **12**), Dangstetten (**13**) and Rheingönheim, Germany (**14**). (Drawing: M.C. Bishop)

Trajan's Column shows how the *pilum* might have been used to help stack equipment when undertaking construction work in the field. The weapon is shown with its butt shoved into the ground; the curved body shield is leant against it, and then the helmet (with its chin strap tied) placed over the *pilum* shank and hanging in front of the shield. One problem with using Trajan's Column in this way is that it was a metropolitan monument which almost certainly depicted scenes with which the sculptors were familiar, rather than (as was once thought) tableaux copied from field sketches produced during Trajan's Dacian Wars of AD 101–02 and AD 105–06. Nevertheless, soldiers were a common sight in Rome, with both the citizen troops and cavalry of the Praetorian Guard and the cavalry of the *equites singulares Augusti* around to serve as models. Therefore, common military practices, such as stacking equipment in this way, may have been noted and used, introducing a note of familiarity for the viewer.

The Later Imperial *pilum*

Changes in provincial funerary practices mean that sculptural evidence for the *pilum* tends to be confined to the city of Rome itself, but the archaeological evidence continues to be found from around the frontiers of the empire.

Much has been made of Vegetius' description of the *spiculum*, which he wrote was the successor to the *pilum*. He may have been confused, however: *spiculum* (literally a point – the same word was used for a bee sting) was in use as a synonym for most types of missile as early as Caesar and regularly appears in writers throughout the Imperial period. This has even produced the notion that Vegetius' *spiculum* was an intermediate stage between the *pilum* and the *angon* (Bongartz 2015: 750), but this appears to run counter to the archaeological and representational evidence, where there is no obvious distinction that would allow the *spiculum* to be isolated archaeologically (*pilum* dimensions vary widely so Vegetius' dimensions are not much help here). It is difficult to avoid the conclusion that the *spiculum* was in fact the *pilum* and that only the name had changed. Much the same thing is observable when the *gladius* was referred to (particularly by poets) as the *ensis*, a word originally used to describe just its tip.

One weapon that does deserve some further attention is the *gaesum*, examples of which are known from a number of later Roman sites in Britain and which – if the identification of the weapon with the artefact is correct (by no means guaranteed) – bears a striking resemblance to the later *angon*. This would presumably retain a direct link back to the Gallic *pila* of the 5th and 4th centuries BC and would in turn suggest an alternative ancestor for the *angon*.

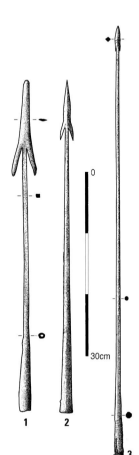

The *gaesum* found at Carvoran, England (**1**), a similar weapon from Nydam in Denmark (**2**) and an *angon* from the Saône River at Le Doubs à Pontoux (**3**). (Drawing: M.C. Bishop)

PREPARING FOR BATTLE

Training

Training with the *pilum* had several distinct stages. Vegetius described the first stage in how recruits were trained in the use of the *pilum*:

> The recruit, who is trained at the stake with the singlestick, is also made to throw spearshafts that are heavier in weight than real javelins at the stake as though at a man. The weapons instructor pays close attention to this: the spearshaft should be twisted with great force, striking with an aimed blow from the missile either at the stake or close by. For both strength of muscle is increased, and knowledge of – and practice in – throwing is acquired by training. (Vegetius, *De Re Militari* 1.14, trans. the author)

The use of dummy weapons for training Roman soldiers was a familiar theme, the practice deriving from gladiatorial drill and the introduction of its methodology into the Roman Army during the Second Punic War. Throwing at a target taught the recruit how to judge distance, but it is

An ox skull from Vindolanda used as target practice by missile weapons with bodkin heads. (Photo: © The Vindolanda Trust)

important to note that the recruit was implicitly being taught to cast the *pilum* at an individual, not at a body of opponents.

The next stage saw mock combat between individuals. For this, rather than just a spear shaft, dummy weapons called *pila praepilata* were used. Opinion differs as to the form these took, but it has been suggested from the name (literally 'ball-tipped *pila*') that regular *pila* with heads blunted in some way were employed. What matters is that they were now being thrown against living targets and not unresponsive wooden stakes: 'On the third day with wooden foils they encountered each other after the manner of a regular battle and hurled missile weapons provided with a button at the end' (Livy, *History of Rome* 26.51.4). Nevertheless, the skills gained in the first stage would be carried over into, and developed in, the second. Regular practice was clearly thought essential, because even emperors, such as Hadrian, might be found doing it: 'He rode and walked a great deal and always kept himself in training by the use of arms (*arma*) and the *pilum*' (*Historia Augusta*, *Hadrian* 26.2). The author of the *Historia Augusta* repeats a similar claim about Aurelian (*Historia Augusta*, *Aurelian* 4.1), perhaps because it was a literary topos for his audience, deliberately recalling Hadrian, who was thought to be a good emperor, or maybe even for both reasons. The distinction between weapons (*arma*) and *pilum* (and javelin) training is found in other writers – such as Cicero and Ovid – and presumably reflects how central exercising with the short sword and shield (which Vegetius refers to as *armatura*: *De Re Militari* 2.14) was to the gladiatorial and military system of training current from the time of Scipio Africanus (236–183 BC).

Other aspects of Roman military training described by Vegetius, notably running, jumping and swimming, are all thought to benefit the modern javelin thrower. Thus a legionary found himself within a training regime that naturally equipped him to be an effective javelineer even before he picked up a practice weapon.

Interestingly, the *Digest* (11.5.2.1) reveals that it was lawful to bet on the results of *pilum*-throwing contests (thereby encouraging *virtus* or courage). At Vindolanda (England), graphic evidence of the nature of Roman target shooting has been found in the form of ox skulls punctured by hits from numerous bodkin-headed missiles, although it is unclear whether these punctures of the ox skulls were produced by *pila* or arrows.

Carriage

Tombstone of Q. Petilius Secundus of *legio XV Primigenia* from Bonn with a *pilum*. (Photo: M.C. Bishop)

The *pilum* was an important part of the legionary persona. Many men, such as Q. Petilius Secundus from *legio XV Primigenia* at Bonn, Germany, are shown on tombstones holding the weapon in the left hand, gripping it just below the expansion, with sword and dagger sheathed. When on the move, the weapon was carried shouldered, unsurprisingly. This is clearly shown on the metopes of the Tropaeum Traiani at Adamclisi, commemorating Trajan's Dacian Wars. When shouldered, the weapon was evidently carried quite high, being held well below the expansion and the bound hand grip illustrated on Frieze A of the Cancelleria reliefs. Some soldiers are even shown with the little finger of the right hand slightly splayed on the Adamclisi reliefs, as if to steady the weapon (an interesting detail, if the metopes were indeed carved by soldiers). The same means of carriage can also be seen on a sculpted column base from the headquarters building of the legionary fortress at Mainz. This shows a legionary and a standard-bearer marching side-by-side. The legionary is again carrying his *pilum* high, with the expansion near his ear, and gripping the shaft near the butt. In contrast, another such pedestal relief, this time showing one legionary advancing behind his shield with his sword drawn, depicts another legionary, shield raised defensively, also with a shouldered *pilum*. This time the weapon is carried much lower, with the expansion on the shoulder. It is possible that the viewer was intended to infer that the first man had cast his javelin but the second still retained his and holds it ready to throw. One of the three Croy Hill legionaries also carries his *pilum* high on his shoulder, not grounded like

those of his companions (but all three men grip the weapon well below the expansion).

When not on the move, fatigued soldiers may often have put their weight on the *pilum* to support themselves. The tendency of camp guards to doze off when leaning on their *pila* is hinted at in an aside by Plutarch, describing preparations for the battle of Pydna in 168 BC: 'He ordered the night watchmen to keep watch without their spears, with the idea that they would be more on the alert and would struggle more successfully

Relief on a column base from the fortress at Mainz showing a legionary with a shouldered *pilum* and a standard-bearer. (Photo: M.C. Bishop)

37

against sleep, if they were unable to defend themselves against their enemies when they approached' (Plutarch, *Aemilius Paullus* 13.7).

Care and maintenance

Every legionary would have been concerned to make sure his *pilum* would not only fly true when cast, but would have been in a suitable condition to be used in hand-to-hand combat, where his life would depend upon it. Precautions taken against corrosion of the iron components are unknown, but experimental evidence suggests that there are viable methods that were available to the Romans, such as blueing or just quenching in olive oil, which inhibit rust (D. Sim, pers. comm.). On the battlefield, however, the soldier would have sought to recover a serviceable weapon after each use, assuming it was possible to do so. Some *pila* will always have landed intact and reusable. Any damage could have been repaired by the legionary himself, if minor, or in the workshop (*fabrica*) if it was more serious, requiring fire-welding, perhaps. Surplus damaged *pila* will also have been recovered for repair or recycling.

Mainz column base relief showing one legionary with a shouldered *pilum* and one with a drawn *gladius.* (Photo: M.C. Bishop)

Pila muralia and fire-pila

There was evidently a type of *pilum* specifically used for defending the ramparts of a fortification when attacked. The *pilum muralium* (or *muralis*) is mentioned by both Caesar and Tacitus in such circumstances. Caesar describes Quintus Cicero's preparations in his besieged camp, noting 'whatever things are required for resisting the assault of the next day are provided during the night: many stakes burned at the end, and a large number of *pila muralia* are procured' (*Gallic War* 5.40.6). Tacitus, describing an uprising in Thrace in AD 26, records how 'The troops, in return, struck them down with spears, dashed them back with their shield-bosses, hurled on them *pila muralia* and piles of massive stone' (*Annals* 4.51).

Modern writers have tended to identify *pila muralia* with the double-ended palisade stakes (*sudes*; sing. *sudis*) carried by legionaries on the march and used to reinforce the defences of encampments. Found at a number of archaeological sites, but most notably the Augustan fortress at Oberaden, as Beeser (1979) and Bennett (1982) have pointed out, these are far too bulky to use as weapons except in extreme circumstances, such as the Batavian siege of the fortress at Vetera (Xanten, Germany) in AD 69–70, when Tacitus describes how 'Some were already in the act of mounting the walls, when the legionaries threw them down with their swords and shields and buried them under a shower of *sudes* and *pila*' (*Histories* 4.23).

One of the more unusual types of archaeological find (and not one attested in the literature) is that of the fire-*pilum*. With hollow heads formed from a basket of two or three strands of iron, these were similar to fire-arrows (*malleoli*) and fire-bolts used by torsion artillery, both of which also occur archaeologically. Although a fire-arrow or -bolt could be used to set fire to a besieged city at a distance, fire-*pila* obviously lacked the range to do this unless used from city walls that had already been taken. Perhaps this gives us a clue to the fact that they were actually used *against* besiegers, being thrown down onto attacking siege engines in the hope of setting them on fire. Thus it is possible that fire-*pila* were in fact the *pila muralia* of which the sources speak. Around 17 fire-*pila* were among the finds from Grad, near Šmihel (Slovenia), a site that has produced a large assemblage of Republican-era weaponry.

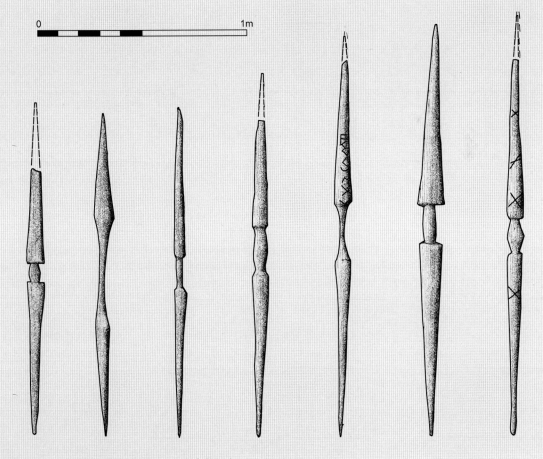

0   1m

Examples of so-called *pila muralia*. (Drawing: M.C. Bishop)

Tombstone of C. Castricius Victor of *legio II Adiutrix* from Budapest (Hungary) showing him holding two *pila*. (Photo: M.C. Bishop)

OPPOSITE Tombstone of C. Valerius Crispus of *legio VIII Augusta* from Wiesbaden showing his one *pilum*. (Photo: M.C. Bishop)

Ownership

Who owned a *pilum*? Was it the legion, the century, or the individual who carried and used it? Stamps are usually an indicator of manufacturer, although none are known from *pila*, while ownership within the Roman Army was indicated by scratched or punched inscriptions made by the individual concerned (again, none are known, because there are so few surviving shafts). Examples of double-ended stakes (often misidentified as *pila muralia*) excavated in the Augustan fortress at Oberaden had centurial inscriptions on them. However, a wooden writing tablet surviving from Carlisle (England) records a cavalry decurion enumerating the missing equipment of his men, and their javelins (*lanceae*) are included within this, listed by individual. Soldiers certainly had to purchase their own equipment from the Army using a kind of hire-purchase scheme, with deductions made at each pay day after recruitment. Thus a soldier probably owned (i.e. had paid for) his two *pila*, but whether he would bother looking for precisely those two after throwing them in battle (rather than the two that needed the least repair!) is a moot point. Plutarch notes that Catulus was able to identify the fallen killed by the *pila* of his men (rather than those of Marius) at the battle of Vercellae in 101 BC 'for these could be known by the name of Catulus which had been cut into the shaft' (Plutarch, *Marius* 27). Whether this was a common practice or not is unknown, as is the true purpose of such identification marks, unless it was to allow for comparison of performance between different commanders' armies. In some ways it echoes the practice of casting commanders' names (and even ribald messages) into lead slingshot during the Republican period.

It has often been supposed that legionaries possessed two *pila* – the assertion is based on both the literary sources (Polybius, *Histories* 6.23.9–11) and representational evidence (the tombstone of C. Castricius Victor from the legionary fortress of Aquincum at Budapest in Hungary shows this). However, it is by no means clear that this was always the case. On his tombstone from Wiesbaden (Germany), C. Valerius Crispus holds only one *pilum*, and the same is true of Q. Petilius Secundus and an unknown legionary from Bonn, while P. Flavoleius Cordus at Mainz likewise has only one weapon. Josephus, in his famous description of the Roman Army of the 1st century AD, only mentions one legionary javelin.

Given the fact that all legionaries were probably keen to retain (or at least replace) their *pila*, it seems likely that the *pilum* used to impale the man at Valencia by the victorious troops of Pompey (see p. 61) was his own weapon.

41

Bending and failure

The *pilum* would often bend. That much is common knowledge, and plenty of examples of bent shanks are known to confirm this and are illustrated within this book; indeed, two out of the three Oberaden *pila*, the most intact examples known, are bent. Nevertheless, it is not invariably true. Experiments conducted by David Sim and the author confirm that, in a straight vertical drop with no sideways momentum, the *pilum* will not bend. However, that was hardly ever the way in which the weapon was used, and scholars have long supposed that the weight of the wooden shaft and its iron shoe would ensure that gravity did its work and bent the shank if it stuck into anything. There were, however, other forces operating on a *pilum* shank that might cause it to bend. If it struck an object (or even the ground) with any lateral moment (so that not all of the energy was being transmitted along the length of the weapon), then it might bend upon impact. Similarly, if used in hand-to-hand combat (as we know it was from reliefs and from texts) then a misplaced thrust or an untimely blow from an opponent might cause the shank to bend. However, during his experiments with throwing *pila*, Peter Connolly (2000: 44–45; 2001/02: 6–7) was unable to reproduce the bending effect. Nevertheless, a sufficiently high proportion of surviving weapons show some sort of bending that there is little room for doubt that it did occur.

So why did the *pilum* bend – was it specifically designed to hamper the shields of an enemy as some writers have suggested? If that was the ultimate intention of the *pilum*, rather than wounding a foe, it was a rather strange purpose with which to imbue a weapon. With a *pilum* stuck in his shield, being encumbered in this way would certainly inspire the enemy to throw away that shield, if he could not remove the offending weapon (and experiment shows both how hard the weapon can be to remove in this way and how this can damage the *pilum*). However, the form of the shank shows that it was clearly designed to follow the head through once it had penetrated a shield and allow the head of the projectile to wound the shield-bearer. Any subsequent bending would certainly be a useful by-product, but it could clearly never have been the primary function of the *pilum*. It should also be remembered that if shields were discarded, further *pila* could then strike unprotected flesh. Like any other weapon, the *pilum* was designed to wound and incapacitate a foe, not just spoil their military equipment.

This much is confirmed by Vegetius, once more: 'However, the infantry army was associated with the missiles called *pila*, with a fine triangular iron point of nine inches [216mm] or a foot [296mm], which fixed in a shield could not be extracted; aimed expertly and with force, it easily penetrated a cuirass; weapons of this type are now rare' (*De Re Militari* 1.20, trans. the author). The reason for the presence of a high proportion of bent metal components in the archaeological record is not difficult to guess – they had been recovered for repair. Experimental archaeology can reveal some of the ways in which *pila* could (but not necessarily did) bend: it provides possibilities rather than definitive answers.

Key to understanding why the *pilum* bent is practical analysis of the damage to the surviving weapon. In the case of the two Hod Hill *pila*, as well as two of the three original Oberaden *pila*, the shanks have primary bends at a point some distance below the head. When a *pilum* misses a target and enters the ground it tends to leave most of its shaft and part of the shank protruding. It is a simple matter for an advancing army to tread these flat to get them out of their way (since they could potentially hinder a retreat, were it needed). Doing this produces exactly the same type of bend as that seen on the Hod Hill and Oberaden *pila* and the weapons offer little resistance to this flattening. All four of these *pila* also exhibit secondary bends nearer the head, and the treading experiment reproduces this too because the shank narrows towards the tip and is weaker. The third Oberaden *pilum*, as well as one from Šmihel, exhibits a bend immediately below the head. This can be reproduced when a *pilum* sticks into, but fails to penetrate fully, a shield board. Attempting to remove the *pilum* (a process which two grown men can find difficult!) can then all too easily lead to such a bend below the head. Indeed, over-eager attempts to remove it, particularly by rocking the *pilum* to free it, could result in fracture of the head, which may explain why heads broken from the shank are so common. Yet another type of damage is present on some of the *pilum* heads from Bar Hill, where the tip is damaged. This might have been caused by striking a stone when entering the ground, but it is also the type of damage that occurs when a shield board is struck a glancing blow that does not result in penetration or even embedding. The important thing to note is that *pila* are unlikely to bend under their own weight when thrown and striking a target or the ground: it is human intervention that is responsible in some way. It is probably in this light that Caesar's comment at the beginning of this book should be read: the *pila* bent when they tried to remove them.

Pilum shanks that seem to have been preserved without any major damage may in fact have required rehafting due to damage to the wooden component, now long decayed. The collection of arms and armour known as the Corbridge Hoard contained bundles of javelins and spears with broken wooden shafts, apparently awaiting rehafting, but this was only apparent because the damaged wooden components were, unusually, preserved. Coincidentally, the Hoard also included a socketed light *pilum* shank with its shank broken below the head.

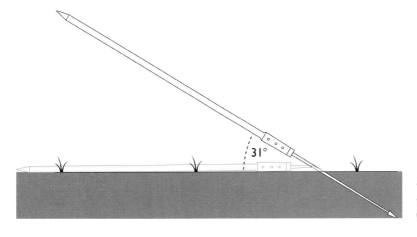

31°

Treading a *pilum* flat, using one of the Oberaden *pila* as an example. (Drawing: M.C. Bishop)

Examples of 3rd-century AD *pilum* heads from the western legionary compound at Corbridge. (Photo: M.C. Bishop)

One of the advantages of an iron (as opposed to steel) shank was that a bent *pilum* could easily be repaired in the field with little in the way of specialist equipment. *Pila* did not just bend, however. *Pilum* shanks are found without heads (as with examples from Alesia), no tangs (like the examples from Hod Hill, both also bent), or even lacking both head and tang (as at Caerleon). Similarly, *pilum* heads that have broken with only a short length of shank attached are common finds, forming the bulk of the *pila* from the rampart-back building at Caerleon. A *pilum* with no head could still be used, as appears to have happened on occasion (as with one of the Oberaden examples), but a broken tang rendered the weapon useless. Thus it is clear that the *pilum* shank could fail beneath the head or above the tang and such failures could only be repaired by a smith with access to a forge. He would have been able to fire-weld a new head or tang onto such a weapon, although it would remain a point of weakness and likely breakage in the future.

Experimental damage to *pila*, showing: a bent head caused by attempting to remove a *pilum* stuck in a shield (**1**); a bent tip resulting from a deflection (**2**); a bent shank following treading down a protruding *pilum* (**3**) – this took just 1 minute 55 seconds to repair to a serviceable state (**4**) with a hammer and anvil. (Photos: M.C. Bishop)

1

2

3

4

IN COMBAT

The *pilum* at a distance

It may seem a strange question to ask about a javelin, but how was a *pilum* thrown? In the modern world, we are used to seeing athletes taking a short run-up before casting their javelin (Olympic regulations state that 30–36.5m is allowed). A legionary in a battle line had no such luxury, however. The weapon obviously had to be cast without disrupting the battle line, so was it done at the run? This seems unlikely, since the soldier then had to draw his sword before contacting the enemy line and drawing a sword at the run is considerably harder than doing it when stationary. Could the *pilum* have been thrown without moving? Again, this might at first glance seem unlikely, for it would have limited the impetus that could be given with movement of the body. Alternatively, a solution involving one or two steps taken before halting, drawing the sword, and only then charging might seem the best compromise (Geyer 1998: 58–59). This at least would allow the weapon time for flight and for disorder to have its maximum effect upon the enemy formation, while also providing some impetus without fragmenting the legionary line. However, given that the legionary traditionally adopted a stance with the shield and left leg advanced (and thus the *pilum* – in the right hand – held back), it might be thought that only one step might have been necessary to help propel the weapon. That one step would then have placed him in the correct stance (right foot forward) for combat with the sword. A second step would have put the legionary on the wrong foot and so a third would then have been necessary, introducing all of the problems with a run-up outlined above.

In fact, in a section probably taken from Cato the Elder (via Celsus), Vegetius helpfully observes: 'Moreover, it should be known that, where missiles are concerned, soldiers must place the left foot in front. For a quivering weapon is thrown with more force like this' (*De Re Militari* 1.20, trans. the author). That seems to imply that no run-up was envisaged. Caesar seems to confirm this when describing how Pompey stopped the front rank of his army advancing into contact at the beginning of the battle of Pharsalus in 48 BC: 'He hoped, too, that the javelins would fall with less effect if the men were kept in their place than if they themselves discharged their javelins and advanced' (*Civil War* 3.92).

Clearly, the *pilum* was envisaged as a short-range weapon and waiting for Caesar's troops to cast, draw swords and advance was seen as reducing the effect of his *pila*. Deliberately withholding a *pilum* volley is also mentioned by both Livy (*History of Rome* 2.30.12) and Frontinus (*Stategemata* 2.1.7) in the context of the consul Verginius' battle against the Volsci in 494 BC when he ordered his men to plant their *pila* in the ground. However, this again seems far too early for the adoption of the *pilum* and it must represent a tradition of this being done with javelins that the sources have subsequently modified to have been *pila*.

If a standing throw was indeed used, then the shield may have been used as a counterbalance. Experimentation shows that the shield does indeed assist in the process if it is raised as the *pilum* is drawn back and then lowered as part of the throw (see p. 46). In this way, no step is

Getting to grips with the *pilum*

The sequence of images depicted opposite – based on representational evidence such as tombstones, Cancelleria Relief A, the Adamclisi metopes and the Croy Hill relief – shows the variety of ways in which the *pilum* could be held. First is the formal stance shown on tombstones and possibly adopted on guard duty, where the weapon is gripped on the binding just below the expansion and the shield is grounded (**1**). When shouldered for the march, the *pilum* is gripped low down the shaft, below the centre of gravity, sometimes splaying the little finger to steady it (**2**). For use in hand-to-hand combat, it was levelled underarm and likewise gripped behind the point of balance (**3**), even for a downward thrust with a reversed grip (**4**).

A possible method for the standing throw is shown in the sequence of images on this page, although there is no representational evidence to substantiate this. Prior to throwing, the *pilum* is held close to the point of balance with the left foot forward and right foot back (**5**). The weapon is then drawn back, lifting the shield to act as a counterbalance, and with the weight on the back foot (**6**), before being launched, at the same time transferring the weight to the left foot as the shield is lowered (**7**), whereupon the sword is drawn ready for use in less time than an enemy requires to close the gap.
(Photos: M.C. Bishop)

5

6

7

5

6

7

necessary, for the weight of the soldier throwing the javelin is transferred from the right (back) to the left (front) foot in the process. While it might be thought that the *pilum* should be held at the point of balance for the optimal throw, tests demonstrate that more force can be imparted by holding the shaft slightly behind the centre of gravity, so that the weapon is very slightly nose-heavy.

An important consideration in all of this is spacing in the formation. A legionary would obviously need enough space behind him to draw his weapon back in order to cast it. With a *pilum* of around 2m in length, held at the point of balance, that might be as much as 2m, in order to avoid striking the man behind him. Polybius describes how the line opened up from a 3Rft (0.89m) to 6Rft (1.78m) spacing to give room for sword fighting (*Histories* 18.30.68), but here he must be referring to lateral spacing, as 3Rft between ranks would not allow enough room to draw the *pilum* back sufficiently before the cast.

The emphasis on quivering or vibration and on imparting an element of rotation occurs frequently in Roman writing in reference to the throwing of javelins. Rotation imparted longitudinal stability during flight – in a more sophisticated form it is found in the rifling of barrels imparting spin to bullets in the gunpowder age. Some modern javelin-throwing theorists still advocate using spin in the shaft during the cast for just this reason.

Experiments in the field by Reinach (1877–1917: 484) and Connolly (2000: 44–45; 2001/02: 6–7) have shown that a range of around 30–40m is achievable with a heavy *pilum*, although 25m seems more like an average. Connolly's reconstructed *hasta velitaris* reached 54.5m, with an estimated average distance of *c*.40m. However, did the Romans attempt to achieve range rather than efficacy? Did they cast upwards to gain distance, or did they prefer to hurl directly at a target at short range? They may even have done both (perhaps explaining why Polybius mentioned that every legionary carried two of them). However, it is clear that there had to be sufficient time for a man to throw his *pilum* and then draw his sword for hand-to-hand combat and this dictated the minimum range: the last thing a front-rank legionary wanted was to be fumbling with his sword and scabbard as the enemy arrived. Given that a world-record sprinter (under ideal conditions) can cover 100m in around 9.5 seconds, a *pilum*-throwing legionary might anticipate at least 2.5 seconds after casting his weapon at an enemy 25m away before their lines made contact. In reality, they may have had that long at 10m, when the target was a shield-encumbered foe advancing over rough terrain. That is easily sufficient time to draw a *gladius*.

Whether the front line dropped unexpended *pila*, passed them back, or stuck the butt in the ground is not recorded, but the first may seem more likely than the other possibilities. A clue comes from Caesar's account of combat around Alesia during his wars in Gaul (58–50 BC): 'Thereupon the enemy joined battle: a shout was raised on both sides, and taken up by an answering shout from the rampart and the whole of the entrenchments. Our troops discarded their *pila* and got to work with their swords' (*Gallic War* 7.88).

Before their confrontation with Boudica, the commander of the Roman forces in Britain, Suetonius Paulinus addressed his troops on the battlefield. In the words of Tacitus (who almost certainly invented the whole thing), the legionaries were told they should be 'keeping their order close, and, when their *pila* were discharged, employing shield-boss and sword, let them

Detail of Adamclisi metope 27 showing a *pilum* with a spherical weight below the expansion. (Photo: C. Chirita)

steadily pile up the dead and forget the thought of plunder: once the victory was gained, all would be their own' (*Annals* 14.36.1). This had the desired effect, so that 'his veteran troops, with the long experience of battle, prepared themselves in a moment to hurl the *pilum*' (Tacitus, *Annals* 14.36.1). The nature of the *pilum* volley against Boudica's troops was evidently a classic example of its kind: 'At first, the legionaries stood motionless, keeping to the defile as a natural protection: then, when the closer advance of the enemy had enabled them to exhaust their missiles with certitude of aim, they dashed forward in a wedge-like formation' (Tacitus, *Annals* 14.37.1). Here are the elements of the stationary throw, in this instance benefiting from an elevated position, aiming at a target, finally followed up with a charge.

Specific instances of sharpshooting with the *pilum* are known. During the siege of Quintus Cicero's camp in Caesar's Gallic campaign of 54 BC, the centurions Vorenus and Pullo vied to outdo each other in deeds of bravery: 'Then, at short range, Pullo sent his *pilum* at the enemy, and pierced one man as he ran forward from the host' (Caesar, *Gallic War* 5.44). During the civil war in Africa in 46 BC, Labienus was confronted by a determined enemy legionary:

> Then said the soldier: 'You'll soon see what I'm made of.' As he spoke the words he flung the helmet from his head so that the other could recognise him and, thus uncovered, brandished his *pilum* with all his force, as he aimed it at Labienus: then plunging it violently full in the horse's chest he said: 'That will teach you, Labienus, that it's a soldier of the Tenth [legion] who is attacking you'. (Caesar, *African War* 16)

There was evidently an art to judging the point of release for a *pilum* volley. Undoubtedly it was along the lines of Israel Puttnam's famous, alleged order at the Battle of Bunker Hill 'don't one of you fire until you see the white of their eyes' but, unlike Puttnam's implicit requirement for individual shooting, the *pilum* volley seems to have required a command. This may be deduced from a passage in Caesar's account of the fighting against Ariovistus' Germans, where he noted: 'Our troops attacked the enemy so fiercely when the signal was given, and the enemy dashed forward so suddenly and swiftly, that there was no time to discharge *pila* upon them. So *pila* were thrown aside, and it was a sword-fight at close quarters' (*Gallic War* 1.52).

Being on the receiving end of a *pilum* volley was a formidable experience, and there are both horrific accounts of the results and a few tales of lucky royal escapes. Plutarch describes how Pyrrhus was wounded by a *pilum* (he uses the Greek word *hyssos*) during the battle of Asculum in 279 BC (*Pyrrhus* 21.9). Later, at the battle of Pydna in 168 BC, according to an account by Poseidonius recorded by Plutarch, the Macedonian king Perseus appears to have been particularly lucky:

> Among the missiles of every sort which were flying on all sides, a javelin made entirely of iron smote him, not touching him with its point, indeed, but coursing along his left side with an oblique stroke, and the force of its passage was such that it tore his tunic and made a dark red bruise upon his flesh, the mark of which remained for a long time. (Plutarch, *Aemilius Paullus* 19.9)

Another Macedonian king, Philip V, suffered a similar near-miss when his horse was killed under him by a Roman *pilum* in battle near Elis in 208 BC (Livy, *History of Rome* 27.32.5).

Pila also proved to be an effective deterrent against elephants in 209 BC when M. Claudius Marcellus fought a series of actions against Hannibal. During the three-day-long battle of Canusium,

> Gaius Decimius Flavus, a tribune of the soldiers, seized a standard from the first maniple [pair of centuries] of the *hastati* and ordered the maniple to which it belonged to follow him. He led them to the spot where the brutes massed together were causing confusion and bade them hurl their *pila* against them. All the weapons stuck fast, for it was not difficult to hit bodies of such size from a short distance and now packed in a dense mass. But although not all were wounded, still those in whose backs the *pila* remained well fixed – so undependable is the species – took to flight and even made the uninjured wheel about. Then no longer did a single maniple hurl its *pila*, but every soldier for himself, provided he was able to catch up with the column of the fleeing elephants. (Livy, *History of Rome* 27.14.7–10)

It is important to note that Hannibal only deployed his elephants against the Roman front line 'when the battle had long been indecisive' (Livy, *History of Rome* 27.14.6), suggesting that the legionaries still retained their *pila* up to this point. This is just one of several incidents that led Zhmodikov (2000) to suggest that *pila* were not always discharged at the beginning of battle but sometimes retained for later use, and this observation is particularly relevant when it comes to discussing the use of the *pilum* in hand-to-hand combat. *Pila* were again employed against elephants during the battle of Zama in 202 BC.

Finally, the quality of the throw could be important if it missed its target. In the modern javelin event, a throw is only measured if the tip strikes the ground; those that land flat or tail first are discounted. A legionary also needed his *pilum* to strike home – preferably into an enemy but, if that did not happen, then tip first into the ground. Experimentation demonstrates that a *pilum* that lands flat or tail first can easily be picked up and returned by a foe.

LEFT Adamclisi metope 31 depicting a legionary stabbing upwards with a *pilum* towards an archer in a tree. The expansion is barely visible but the *pilum* head can be made out near the archer's left shoulder. (Photo: C. Chirita)

RIGHT Adamclisi metope 35 showing a legionary standing in a Dacian waggon stabbing downwards with his *pilum*, the expansion being just visible above the warrior's right shoulder. (Photo: C. Chirita)

The *pilum* up close

The earliest Roman *pila* were purely used as javelins, as Polybius suggests in his description of the battle of Telamon in 225 BC: 'The tribunes therefore distributed among the front lines the spears of the *triarii* who were stationed behind them, ordering them to use their swords instead only after the spears were done with' (*Histories* 2.33.4). The *principes* and the *hastati* of the front two lines of a Republican legion were normally armed with *pila*, while the *triarii* in the rear had spears. The barbed-headed *pila* of the time do not appear to have been thought suitable for use as thrusting spears, hence the need to reassign weapons. The later *pilum* was, however, quite capable of being used in this way in hand-to-hand combat. This is shown quite dramatically on the metopes from the Tropaeum Traiani at Adamclisi, with one legionary, standing on a cart, thrusting his *pilum* overarm and downwards into a Dacian right up to the wooden expansion of the shaft. Less certainly, another legionary is depicted thrusting his javelin underarm at a Dacian equipped with a bow and arrow, crouching in a tree.

The *pilum* up close (opposite)

Republican legionaries storm the ramparts of the hillfort at Grad near Šmihel (Slovenia) at some point near the end of the 3rd/beginning of the 2nd centuries BC. Here, *pila* are being used at close quarters as well as in a preparatory volley. A heavy *hastatus* prepares to cast a tanged *pilum*, while the *velis* (skirmisher) next to him has a socketed *hasta velitaris* (a light form of *pilum*). During the 2nd century BC, the *hastati* and *principes* of the first and second legionary ranks began to change their small metal breastplates for the additional protection offered by the mail already worn by the *triarii* of the third rank.

Writing under Augustus, Strabo is unequivocal in attributing two roles to the *pilum*: 'For the spear is used in two ways, one in hand-to-hand combat and the other for hurling like a javelin; just as the pike serves both purposes, for it can be used both in close combat and as a missile for hurling, which is also true of the *sarissa* and the *pilum* (*hyssos*)' (*Geography* 10.1.12).

Two frequently cited passages describe this method of use of the *pilum*. Plutarch's account of Marc Antony's troops encountering the Parthians includes this: 'But the Romans, with a full battle cry, suddenly sprang up, and thrusting with their *pila* slew the foremost of the Parthians and put all the rest to rout' (*Antony* 45.3). Plutarch, like Dionysius of Halicarnassus, Polybius and Strabo before him, used the Greek word *hyssos* to identify the *pilum*. He also recounts their use as thrusting spears against Pompey's cavalry by Caesar's legionaries at Pharsalus:

> Before they could attack, the cohorts ran out from where Caesar was posted, not hurling their *pila*, as usual, nor yet stabbing the thighs and legs of their enemies with them, but aiming them at their eyes and wounding their faces. They had been instructed to do this by Caesar, who expected that men little conversant with wars or wounds, but young, and pluming themselves on their youthful beauty, would dread such wounds especially, and would not stand their ground, fearing not only their present danger, but also their future disfigurement. And this was what actually came to pass; for they could not endure the upward thrust of the *pila*, nor did they even venture to look the weapon in the face, but turned their heads away and covered them up to spare their faces. (Plutarch, *Caesar* 45.2–4)

Elsewhere, Plutarch notes: 'Whenever the cavalry charged, they were to run out through the front ranks, and were not to hurl their *pila*, as the best soldiers usually did in their eagerness to draw their swords, but to strike upwards with them and wound the faces and eyes of the enemy' (*Pompey* 69.3).

A document written by Flavius Arrianus, governor of Cappadocia under the Emperor Hadrian, anticipates much the same manner of use for the weapon. Purporting to be a battle plan in case of invasion by the steppe nomad Alani, it includes instructions for how his legions were to meet a charge by the enemy cavalry:

> And the front four ranks of the formation must be of spearmen, whose spear points end in thin iron shanks. And the foremost of them should hold them at the ready, in order that when the enemies near them, they can thrust the iron points of the spears at the breast of the horses in particular. Those standing in the second, third and fourth rank of the formation must hold their spears ready for thrusting if possible, wounding the horses and killing the horsemen and put the rider out of action with the spear stuck in their heavy body armour and the iron point bent because of the softness. The following ranks should be of the javelineers. (Arrian, *Ektaxis kata Alanoon* 17, trans. Sander van Dorst)

Adamclisi metope 44 showing legionaries advancing with their *pila* levelled horizontally, with the weapons gripped well behind the centre of gravity. (Photo: C. Chirita)

The Greek word for 'spear' used by Arrian is not *hyssos*, but rather *kontos*, although there seems little room for doubt that it refers to the *pilum*, with its references to thin, bending, iron shanks. Here, Arrian has quite deliberately changed one of the principles of legionary combat in order to counter a cavalry army. It is unlikely that there would be sufficient time to judge a *pilum* volley correctly in the face of a swift cavalry charge, anyway. The commonplace is that cavalry cannot

The *pilum* in formation (overleaf)

Hadrianic legionaries arrayed in battle order according to the instructions of the commander of the army of Cappadocia, Flavius Arrianus. Preparing to receive the mounted Alani, the front four legionary ranks hold their *pila* at the ready for use as thrusting spears. Behind them, the next four ranks are ready to throw their *pila* over the heads of the font ranks. At the back, archers will shoot over all their heads. The legionaries wear a range of equipment that would be found at the time, including one or two very old pieces.

penetrate a close, resolute infantry line, as demonstrated by the British squares at Waterloo and repeated later in the 19th century in the writings of Ardant du Picq. Arrian relied on the legionaries' ability to stand up to the charge and the horses' reluctance to face four ranks of levelled *pila*.

Legionaries are also depicted with levelled *pila* on two of the surviving Adamclisi metopes. One is very badly weathered but the other is sufficiently clear to make it certain that *pila* are depicted on one and likely on the other. However, it is debatable whether movement is being depicted, or whether a battle line is in fact being shown with the legionaries in the classic 'at the ready' pose with left foot advanced behind the shield. This relief may even be seen to suggest that *pila* were used underarm when thrusting, although the soldiers may conceivably be about to raise their javelins in order to cast them, but it is noteworthy that they are again gripped well behind the point of balance, as if to maximize their length for thrusting (they would have to be gripped at or near the point of balance for throwing).

Vegetius, having discussed throwing *pila*, then talks about using them in close combat: 'But when it comes 'to the *pila*', as they say, in hand-to-hand sword fighting, soldiers must have the right foot forward, so that both flanks are protected from the enemy and they cannot be wounded, and the right hand is to the fore, in order to deliver a blow' (*De Re Militari* 1.20, trans. the author). Whether the spear was used under- or overarm is a perennial source of debate – particularly among re-enactors – when discussing ancient armies, even though the representational evidence for the Roman period is unequivocal in showing the *hasta* being used overarm. The cavalry *contus*, held two-handed, was used underarm and the Adamclisi metopes suggest that the *pilum* was also used in this way in hand-to-hand combat, held in the right hand and behind the point of balance. The metopes are widely accepted as having been sculpted by soldiers, so are comparatively reliable iconographic evidence.

Gripped behind the centre of gravity, in the manner suggested by the representational evidence, as much as 1.5m of a 2m-long *pilum* may have protruded in front of the hand of the soldier. When the blade of the *gladius Hispaniensis* of the Republican period did not exceed 0.8m (and subsequent swords were even shorter), this gave the legionary a formidable reach in comparison. Using the *pilum* in this way may have wrong-footed an enemy expecting a volley of javelins, then hand-to-hand combat against short swords, but there is another dimension to this altogether. There was evidently some debate among the Romans as to whether it was better to chop or stab with the *gladius*, manifested in the text of Vegetius, who used a variety of sources to compile his *De Re Militari* and ended up arguing forcefully both for and against chopping as a result. Using the *pilum* as a stabbing weapon accords with the school of thought that the most effective way of fighting was to thrust, not cut. As Vegetius noted when writing of the sword (in a section probably ultimately derived from the Roman military writer Julius Frontinus, who had himself commanded Roman armies), 'a cut, should it be delivered

with any force whatsoever, frequently does not kill, when the vital parts are defended by equipment and bone. On the contrary, a point brought to bear is fatal at two [Roman] inches [49mm]; for it inevitably penetrates whatever vital parts it is stuck into' (*De Re Militari* 1.12, trans. the author). Presumably the targets preferred for stabbing blows with the *gladius* were also prioritized when the *pilum* was used in this manner. Writing of training recruits at the stake with the sword, Vegetius notes: 'he might aim for the head or face, then he is threatened from the sides, then he strained to cut down at the hams and shins' (*De Re Militari* 1.11, trans. the author).

Targeting the face was of course precisely what Caesar had ordered his legionaries to do against Pompey's cavalry, thereby using the additional reach of the *pilum* to the greatest advantage. None of the sources makes it clear whether the shield was used offensively alongside the *pilum*, as it was with the *gladius*, but it seems likely, since this complementary pairing of weapons was so integral to the legionary *armatura*.

Finally, archaeology bears witness to one of the more gruesome uses of the *pilum*. After the city of Valentia (modern Valencia) was captured from the rebel army of Q. Sertorius by Pompey's troops in 75 BC, the victorious legionaries exacted their revenge on Sertorius' troops. Amidst evidence of amputations and other brutal post-capture acts, one excavated skeleton of a mature adult male was found impaled on a *pilum*.

As Strabo observed, the *pilum* was more than just a javelin, although its use in close combat appears to have developed as the weapon itself evolved.

Mature adult male skeleton from Valencia impaled upon a *pilum*. (Photo: SIAM. Ajuntament de Valencia)

Detail of the funerary altar of C. Firmidius Rufus of *cohors VI Praetoria* from Aquileia, Italy, showing (top left) his *gladius*, (centre) his helmet and shield and (right) his *pilum* and *pugio*. (Photo: J.C.N. Coulston)

WHERE DID ALL THE *PILA* GO?

The *pilum* does not normally occur in excavated Roman burials. Weapons burial was rare in the Roman period anyway, although some auxiliary troops did occasionally practise it (Bishop & Coulston 2006: 33–34). A wide range of other military equipment is recovered from funerary contexts but, like the curved, rectangular shield bosses of legionary shields, this does not include *pila*. This is only to be expected if the *pilum* was indeed exclusively used by the citizen troops of the legions in the provinces and the praetorian and urban cohorts in the city of Rome. There was also a financial incentive that tended to ensure burial did not happen: troops had to buy their equipment from the Army upon enlistment and, over time, this represented a considerable investment. When soldiers retired or died, the value of the weapons they had purchased was refunded by the Army, who could then pass them on to new recruits.

The bulk of *pilum* finds from the archaeological record comprises weapons that had been kept for repair or scrapping. This explains why so many pieces were broken or bent. Occasionally they are found in battlefield contexts, presumably because they were not recovered at the time. There would be an imperative on both sides in a conflict to recover spent *pila*: even a foe who did not habitually employ the *pilum* would find them a valuable resource, since they could reforge the iron into something else. *Pila* from Alesia, Kalkriese and Harzhorn fall into this category of battlefield losses.

Sometimes, however, *pila* are recovered more or less intact from watery contexts. This often occurs in areas where prehistoric and early medieval finds are found and may have derived from votive offerings (Bishop & Coulston 2006: 30–31). Archaeologists frequently exhibit mild desperation when resorting to 'ritual' as an explanation for a phenomenon, but votive deposits of weaponry are well-attested by inscriptions and formed part of the contract religion favoured by the Army, whereby good outcomes were believed to be ensured by the promise of an offering. A centurion of *legio III Cyrenaica* dedicated a shield and javelin (*scutum et lancea*) at Tongres (Belgium) and, since troops owned their weapons, they were free to dispose of them as they saw fit (so long as they purchased a replacement). Weapons from watery sites include the unprovenanced *pilum* illustrated on this page (recovered with absolutely no surface corrosion, indicating that it lay in anaerobic conditions), as well as items from the Saône in France and the Rhine at Mainz. There is also a socketed *pilum* shank (lacking its head) from a temple site at Empel in the Netherlands.

CONCLUSIONS

The *pilum* was a weapon unique to the legions and the praetorian and urban cohorts in Rome. As such, it was instantly recognizable as belonging to citizen troops. Along with the curved body shield and, under the Republic and Early Empire, the short sword, it was part of a package of equipment that was found to be reliable in the hands of well-trained heavy infantry. It was versatile – not only could it deliver a withering volley at short range in order to disorganize an enemy immediately before engaging in hand-to-hand combat, but it could also be used as a thrusting spear when occasion demanded, particularly at the behest of gifted and imaginative commanders. Paradoxically, its main faults were its chief advantages: it broke easily and was difficult for an enemy to reuse. At the same time it could usually be repaired without too much difficulty. It was not, however, a disposable weapon. Too much effort was needed in its manufacture for a unit to be able to discard *pila* in large numbers after a battle. Expended weapons would have to have been retrieved and patched up ready for combat in the future. In this way, the *pilum* was the ultimate recyclable weapon.

Three views of an extremely well-preserved, unprovenanced *pilum* from a watery environment, formerly in the Guttmann Collection and now privately owned. (Photos: A. Pangerl)

IMPACT
More than just a javelin

TACTICAL INFLUENCE

Modern writers have suggested that the *pilum* was fundamental to the development of Roman legionary tactics, notably the manipular system, whereby the previously monolithic Roman Army began to employ sub-units – the *manipuli* or maniples – in the field. It is sometimes suggested that the early Roman Army was based on a hoplite phalanx, using equipment derived from or inspired by the Greek city states in Italy, possibly at one remove through the Etruscans (the earliest Roman kings traditionally being thought of as Etruscan). The idea of a change in tactics arriving at the same time as the large body shield and *pilum* were adopted is obviously attractive, but where is the evidence?

Part of our problem – arguably a major part – is that the evidence is so scarce. The assumption that the early Roman Army used a phalanx system resembling that employed by the Greek city states is founded upon a resemblance in the equipment, notably the round hoplite shield together with a Greek-style sword. If that assumption is flawed, which is not impossible, then the evolution into the manipular system in the 4th century BC may not have been as radical as is sometimes thought. Nevertheless, it seems inescapable that the body shield and heavy javelin had a significant role to play. The hoplite style of combat centred around the use of the thrusting spear and shield, whereas the javelin enabled a devastating, short-range missile volley to become an important preliminary to hand-to-hand combat using the sword: battle became more intimate. These two components in the new Roman fighting style were inevitably linked to the equipment being used, but it is not immediately obvious whether the equipment produced the tactics, or the tactics led to the adoption of new weaponry.

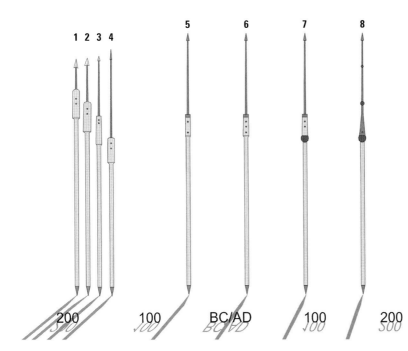

Timeline showing the development of Roman *pila* with the Telamon (**1**), Šmihel (**2**, **3**), Ephyra (**4**), Renieblas (**5**), Oberaden (**6**), weighted (**7**) and Later Imperial (**8**) types.(Drawing: M.C. Bishop)

If Rome's enemies were unfamiliar with this tactic (and most were) it gave the Roman Army of the 4th century BC a considerable advantage on the battlefield. The thrusting spear was not entirely relinquished, for at the time Polybius was writing (in the mid-2nd century BC), although the *principes* and *hastati* of a legion were armed with the *pilum*, the *triarii* at the rear still used the thrusting spear. This was during a period when archaeological examples of the *pilum* conform to Polybius' description by having a large, barbed head. Later in the Republican period, the head changed into the familiar pyramidal, bodkin form, with a longer shank than before. That this was thought suitable for use as a thrusting spear is apparent from the sources, so it may be that this evolution in the form of the weapon was connected with the replacement of the spear with the *pila* among the rear ranks, either as a contributory factor or as a result of it.

Countering the salvo of heavy javelins was difficult. The Parthians achieved it against Crassus' force at Carrhae in 53 BC by refusing to engage the legionary force at close range, but rather using horse archers to wear down the Roman heavy infantry. This was easier for a mobile cavalry force to achieve than for infantry armies. Nevertheless, various commanders showed that the *pilum* volley was not invincible and some could even turn it to their advantage.

At Trasimene (217 BC), Hannibal used the element of surprise against the Romans and they do not appear to have had the chance to launch a coordinated *pilum* volley against their attackers. At Cannae (216 BC), he placed Spanish and Celtic troops opposite the Roman legionaries. These then, although seemingly sacrificed as '*pilum* fodder', apparently did not receive the customary *pilum* volley – it is not even mentioned by Polybius or Livy but Appian supplies the information that a headwind meant the Romans were unable to throw them (*Hannibal* 22).

UNDERSTANDING THE *PILUM*

One of the stranger by-products of the *pilum* is the effect it had on scholars in the 19th and 20th centuries. A string of learned works by the likes of Wylie (1870), Lindenschmit (1881; 1882) and Dahm (1895) appeared trying to make sense of the classical sources, sometimes with little or no recourse to actual archaeological evidence. One of the first, the German Köchly, was almost lyrical in his admiration, stating in 1863 (perhaps a little hyperbolically) that the *pilum*, together with the *gladius*, conquered the world for the Romans. In Reinach's entry on the *pilum* for Daremberg and Saglio's *Dictionnaire des antiquités grecques et romaines*, archaeological finds (notably from the work sponsored by Napoléon III at Alise-Sainte-Reine, believed to be the ancient Alesia) were beginning to feed into the text- and representation-based discussions that had gone before. Such studies led on to the debate about origins already mentioned (see p. 7).

Status symbol

The iconic status of the *pilum* should not be underestimated. Legionaries and praetorians carry it on their tombstones alongside the curved body shield, symbolic of their status as citizen soldiers. Like the *gladius*, Tacitus used it in his famous description of the attack on the stronghold of Caratacus to distinguish legionary troops from auxiliaries: 'if they offered a resistance to the auxiliaries, they were struck down by the *gladii* and *pila* of the legionaries; if they faced against the legionaries, they fell under the *spathae* and *hastae* of the auxiliaries' (*Annals* 12.35).

The distinctiveness of the *pilum* as a weapon of citizen soldiers like legionaries and praetorians is clear from both representational evidence (most notably tombstones) and the texts. Tacitus was clear about such distinctions (e.g. *Histories* 1.38), while Seneca, writing on the effects of anger, suggested that one of its effects was that 'legions aim their *pila* at their commander' (*On Anger* 3.2.4), the association of the two being implicit.

Funerary altar of Q. Flavius Crito and Q. Flavius Proculus of the *cohors XII Urbana* in the Vatican Museum, Rome, depicting Proculus with a multi-weighted *pilum*. (Photo: J.C.N. Coulston)

However, despite the evident significance of the *pilum*, scholars have periodically expressed doubts that there was a distinction between legionary and auxiliary equipment. This has been partly inspired by the discovery of *pila* and segmental body armour (a citizen-soldier indicator on Trajan's Column) during the excavation of sites that were supposed to have held auxiliary garrisons. In fact, the heavy *pilum* was clearly suited to heavy, close-order infantry use and inappropriate to the skirmishing roles undertaken by auxiliary infantry. The supposition that a site was designed to hold a particular force is often based on weak and unsatisfactory evidence and, most importantly, a misunderstanding of the way in which garrisoning worked (Bishop 1999). In Tacitus' description of the key battle of Mons Graupius in AD 83 or 84, won by Agricola's auxiliary troops rather than his legionary infantry, it is difficult to know if it is significant that there is no mention of *pila* (*Agricola* 36).

Politics and the *pilum*

There was a darker, symbolic side to the *pilum*. Just as it was paired with the *gladius* on the battlefield, so they came to participate in Roman politics, especially in the troubled times of the latter part of the 2nd and early 3rd centuries AD. Where the *gladius* was used to decapitate political or military rivals, then the *pilum* could be used to display the resulting grisly trophy. This is exactly what happened to Pescennius Niger in AD 197 after he was killed by his rival to the purple, Septimius Severus (*Historia Augusta*, *Severus* 9.1; *Niger* 6.1). If the *Historia Augusta* is to be believed, the same fate befell Severus' other rival, the usurper Clodius Albinus (*Historia Augusta*, *Albinus* 9.6), although the coincidence of events and even the language used may suggest a literary 'echo', with one original event being attributed to two separate occasions. Antoninus Diadumenianus and his father, Opellius Macrinus, apparently met a similar end (*Historia Augusta*, *Diadumenianus* 9.4). Either the author of the *Historia Augusta* (whose particular conceit was to pretend the work was written by several different authors) was making this all up, or a new use for the *pilum* had not only been found but was briefly to become fashionable.

Relief depicting praetorians, probably from the Arch of Claudius, showing *pilum* shanks belonging to the two men in low relief in the background. (Photo: J. Jännick)

Although there was a ban on weapons being carried by soldiers within the city of Rome itself, this does not seem to have applied to the Praetorian Guard, although they did conceal their swords beneath togas when on palace guard duty. The soldiers depicted on Cancelleria Relief A, generally accepted to be praetorians (although they carry no insignia to mark them as such), are equipped with *pila*. This may be explicable if the scene was, as has been suggested by some scholars, intended to depict Domitian's departure for his war against the Chatti in Germania. The same is true of the soldiers on a relief in the Louvre, often interpreted as praetorians and now believed to derive from the Arch of Claudius erected after his victory in Britain, where *pila* are shown. They also occur on praetorian tombstones and on those of members of the urban cohorts.

Words and weaponry

The story of the terminology of *pila* is not as straightforward as it might seem. The terms used within the Roman Army – and most particularly by writers on the subject, often seeking literary or dramatic effect – were fluid and often contradictory. Aulus Gellius, a 2nd-century AD writer of a light, literary confection, reveals something of the difficulties in being too dogmatic terminologically:

> Once upon a time, when I was riding in a carriage, to keep my mind from being dull and unoccupied and a prey to worthless trifles, it chanced to occur to me to try to recall the names of weapons, darts and swords which are found in the early histories, and also the various kinds of boats and their names. Those, then, of the former that came to mind at the time are the following: spear (*hasta*), javelin (*pilum*), fire-pike (*phalarica*), half-javelin (*semiphalarica*), iron javelin (*soliferrea*), Gallic spear (*gaesa*), javelin (*lancea*), hunting-darts (*spari*), javelins (*rumices*), long bolts (*trifaces*), barbed-javelins (*tragulae*), German spears (*frameae*), thonged-javelins (*mesanculae*), Gallic bolts (*cateiae*), broadswords (*rumpiae*), poisoned arrows (*scorpii*), Illyrian hunting-spears (*sibones*), cimeters (*siciles*), darts (*veruta*), swords (*enses*), daggers (*sicae*), broadswords (*machaerae*), double-edged swords (*spathae*), small-swords (*lingulae*), poniards (*pugiones*), cleavers (*clunacula*). (Aulus Gellius, *Attic Nights* 10.25.1–2)

In his commentary on Virgil's *Aeneid*, Servius is quite clear on his definitions: '*pila*, along with *pilum*, is properly the Roman spear, as the *gaesa* is Gallic, or the *sarissa* Macedonian' (*Aeneid* 7.664). Not only could specific words be used for particular weapons, however, as there were euphemisms to which resort could be made for stylistic purposes. So, while legionaries had *pila* and auxiliaries (and, by the 3rd century AD, some legionaries too!) *lanceae*, both could be described by writers as *missilis* (the very obvious root of the English word 'missile') and *tela* (more generally 'weapons').

The function of the *pilum* was even used as a metaphor by one Republican-era playwright. Plautus (writing in the late 3rd and early 2nd centuries BC) refers to a catapult bolt as a *pilum catapultarium* (*Curculio* 689), which serves to illustrate how both weapons may have been considered to share an armour-piercing intent. We can only wonder whether Roman soldiers made play on the fact that the same word, *spiculum*, could be used for their javelin and the sting of a bee or wasp.

Roman writers loved etymology, although modern scholarship suggests that many, perhaps most, of their derivations were simply wrong. Varro (*De Lingua Latina* 5.116) believed *pilum* to derive from *perilum*, because it killed the enemy! The word *pilum* is now thought to be a

Decoration and display

The *pilum* was not entirely unadorned. While it was by no means crudely finished, as the Oberaden examples demonstrate, there was no reason for the smith to expend valuable time finishing its metal components to a shine when it took so long just to produce the shank. That is not to say the owner may not have sat with some abrasive and polished his personal javelin. Ancient texts often comment on the sunlight glinting off the weaponry of an army and arriving at a battle with gleaming weapons was certainly seen as a tactic to dent the morale of an opponent. One detail that is preserved by Cancelleria Relief A is that the spherical weight added just below the expansion seems to have been decorated (on praetorian weapons, at least). This appears to take the form of an embossed eagle with its wings raised, clutching Jupiter's thunderbolt between its talons. Such decoration can have served no practical purpose, so must have been purely for appearance. Later *pila* are shown on tombstones to have had some sort of spiral binding or perhaps painted motif running all the way down to the butt. Decorated spear shafts are known from Germanic contexts and this practice may have been adopted by the Roman Army too.

In victory, *pila* might be adorned with laurel wreaths (a practice which is depicted on the Great Trajanic Frieze). Writing about the laurel, Pliny the Elder notes: 'For the Romans more particularly it is the messenger of joyful tidings, and of victory: it accompanies the despatches of the general, and it decorates the javelins and *pila* of the soldiers and the *fasces* which precede their chief' (Pliny, *Natural History* 15.40). The symbolism inherent in such decoration explains the significance attached to instances of St Elmo's Fire manifested around *pila* (Dionysius of Halicarnassus, *Roman Antiquities* 5.46.2).

A *pilum* decorated with a laurel wreath depicted on the Great Trajanic Frieze incorporated into the Arch of Constantine. (Photo: J.C.N. Coulston)

secondary meaning derived from the same word used for a pestle. This in turn led to some rather strange reconstructions of the *pilum* in the 19th century which attempted to match the weapon with the utensil, with results that were more amusing than practical.

There was a vocabulary specific to and derived from *pilum* usage, typified by Plautus' metaphorical use of the phrase *pilum iniecisti* ('I have launched an attack': *Mostellaria* 3.1.43).

The Roman Army may also have adopted terms derived from the word *pilum* to signify formations and ranks. The *antepilani* was a term given to the *principes* and *hastati* because – according to Livy (*History of Rome* 8.8.7–8) – they were stationed ahead of the front ranks (*pili*) of the *triarii*. This explanation seems somewhat contrived (as well as inconsistent with the position of the *primus pilus*, or senior centurion, within Imperial legionary deployments) and it may just derive from the fact that it refers to the *pilum*-armed troops (*pilani*) in the front part of the formation (*ante*). As ever, Livy's distance from the period about which he was writing makes certainty impossible. Nevertheless, the translation of *primus pilus* as 'first spear' so beloved of historical-fiction authors may yet contain an element of truth in it.

Unlike the *gladius*, the *pilum* has even left its mark on modern English. The word 'pile' survives for a missile or dart, the *Oxford English Dictionary* noting that it was first recorded in the Old English poem *Vainglory*, preserved in a 10th-century manuscript in the *Codex*

Exoniensis. Here the phrase 'Bið þæt æfþonca eal gefylled feondes fligepilum facensearwum' can be found in line 26 ('that vexation is completely filled with envious thoughts by the fiend's flying darts'). Although the weapon itself did not last into the medieval period, its Roman name did.

DERIVATIVES

Vegetius, who was probably writing in the 4th century AD, knew of a weapon 'which they called *pilum* and is now known as the *spiculum*' (*De Re Militari* 2.15.5, trans. the author). The *spiculum* is also mentioned, but not described, by the 4th-century AD historian Ammianus Marcellinus. However, Ammianus still writes about the *pilum* (27.2.3), so it had not disappeared completely. Moreover, the non-specificity of terms like *spiculum*, which just means 'little point', meant it could be and was used as a catch-all term for javelins and other missiles.

Vegetius also comments upon the *bebra*, which he mentions in the context of describing the *pilum* used by 'barbarian' troops: 'However, barbarian infantry with shields are especially associated with what they call "*bebrae*", and they carry two or even three in battle' (*De Re Militari* 1.20, trans. the author). Vegetius is the only source for the term *bebra* (it is not included in Aulus Gellius' list). The legacy of the *pilum* continued into the Byzantine period, although not necessarily within Roman forces. The Frankish *angon* is described by the 6th-century AD writer Agathias:

> They are armed with double axes and *angones* [spears] with which they do most execution. These *angones* are of a length that may be both used as a javelin or in close fight against a charge of the enemy. The staff of this weapon is covered with iron laminae or hoops, so that but very little wood appears, even down to the spike at the butt-end. On either side of the head of this javelin are certain barbs projecting downward close together as far as the shaft. The Frank soldier, when engaged with the enemy, casts his *angon*, which, if it enters the body, cannot be withdrawn in consequence of the barbs. Nor can the weapon be disengaged if it pierce the shield, for the bearer of the shield cannot cut it off because of the iron plates with which the staff is defended, while the Frank rushing forward jumps upon it as it trails on the ground, and thus bearing down his antagonist's defence, cleaves his skull with his axe, or transfixes him with a second javelin. (Agathias, *Histories* 5.2.4–8)

The similarities of both function and form between *pilum* and *angon* are readily apparent in this piece and are further confirmed by actual archaeological examples of the weapon. Ludwig Lindenschmit, who had an interest in the *pilum* (see p. 72), also described several examples of the *angon* from Germany, which include barbs forced in close to the head 'as if they had been forced through some solid body'; he also noted that 'the examples from Wiesbaden and Darmstadt are also bent as if they have been employed in warfare' (quoted in Akerman 1855: 79). Interestingly, all of the examples illustrated by Lindenschmit were socketed and at least one of them seems to have been ritually 'killed', rather than bent in combat.

The word 'angon' was originally Greek (ἄγγων) and was taken into the Frankish tongue as ango and Anglo-Saxon as anga. Although it is often said to be largely Frankish in the 6th century AD, examples were found in the ship burial at Sutton Hoo and as grave goods elsewhere in Britain (Underwood 1999). It may also appear in a fragmentary Anglo-Saxon poem called the *Waldere* about a Frankish warrior, although there is some doubt about the text at this point (Himes 2009). By the 8th century AD, the weapon had faded from popularity (Schnurbein 1974).

FALSE POSITIVES

Not all artefacts recovered from the archaeological record that look like a *pilum* necessarily were such. Although most catapult bolts with pyramidal heads were socketed, a proportion of them in the early Imperial period had a more complex structure, whereby a separate,

False positives: (from left to right) a pyramidal arrowhead and composite catapult bolt, both from Windisch, and an awl and a drill bit-head, both from London. (Drawing: M.C. Bishop)

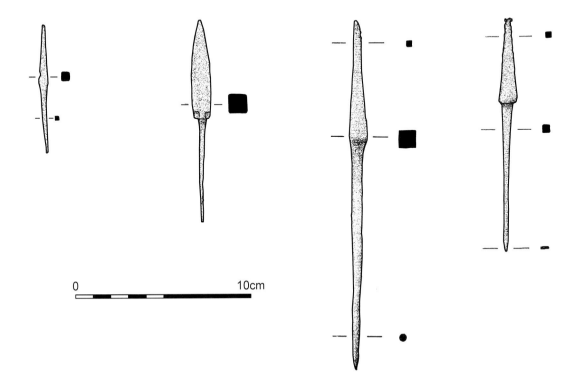

0   10cm

hardwood cap was fitted to the main shaft and a pyramidal, tanged iron head inserted into the end of that hardwood section. Such tanged heads can, when corroded, look like a broken *pilum* head. Both *pilum* and catapult bolt shared the same purpose – penetrating armour (hence Plautus' description of a catapult bolt as a *pilum catapultarium*). The *pilum* achieved this through mass at short range, the catapult bolt by velocity at a distance. Hence they were both equipped with bodkin or pyramidal heads.

The tanged bodkin head was also used on some arrows and, although generally smaller than *pilum* heads, these can sometimes be confused for the genuine article.

Two final categories of item that can occasionally be mistaken for the *pilum* are both tools: the awl and the bit-head from a drill. In short, not everything that looks like a *pilum* is one!

MODERN RECONSTRUCTIONS

Reinach was already building *pilum* replicas in order to test them in the 1870s. However, he was hampered by having access to only a limited amount of archaeological evidence which inevitably conflicted with the rather muddled classical sources. One of the first carefully researched museum replicas of the *pilum* is that equipping the Roman soldier model produced by Ludwig Lindenschmit for his new Römisch-Germanische Zentralmuseum in Mainz, where it can still be seen. Lindenschmit had written about the *pilum* in both his *Alterthümer unserer heidnischen Vorzeit* of 1881 and his *Tracht und Bewaffnung des römischen Heeres während der Kaiserzeit* (the first serious study of Roman arms and armour) a year later, so he knew the evidence well. His model was largely based on the tombstone of C. Valerius Crispus of *legio VIII Augusta* from Wiesbaden (which he had illustrated in *Tracht und Bewaffnung*).

Nowadays, serviceable replicas of the *pilum* abound. These are mainly designed to supply the re-enactor market and are almost exclusively modelled upon the Oberaden *pila*. Metal components tend to be fashioned from easily obtainable mild steel, while the wooden shaft is cut down from timber, rather than formed from stronger, coppiced wood (an easy way to tell this is that cut-down timber displays the stripes of tree rings which, on a coppiced pole, can only be seen by cutting through it). Such replicas therefore look like *pila*, but it is questionable whether they can ever function in quite the same way as those made according to the original methods and materials. To expect them to do so is to miss the point, however: they are only really intended to *look like pila*. Reconstructions made for experimental purposes, such as those produced by Peter Connolly, are a different matter altogether. Careful attention to the use of materials that are as authentic as possible, together with basing the forms on published archaeological examples, produces the best results. Nevertheless, the chief principle of experimental archaeology must always be borne in mind: it can only ever show what *might have* happened, not what *did* happen.

Modern reconstruction of an Oberaden *pilum*. (Photo: M.C. Bishop)

CONCLUSION

REPLACED

The *pilum* lasted longer in legionary service than the *gladius*. Even then, the imitations such as the *angon* show that it was still admired in some quarters, presumably for the same reasons it was adopted by the Romans in the first place. It was an essential part of the 'legionary package' of javelin, sword and shield: a winning combination which the Romans retained for understandable reasons.

The *plumbata* was the replacement for the *pilum*. Described by Vegetius (who also called it the *martiobarbulus/mattiobarbulus*) and the anonymous author of the *De Re Bellicis*, it had a barbed head and a socketed iron shank fixed to a short wooden shaft, onto which was attached a lead weight. Each legionary carried several of these on the inside of his shield. What made these missiles so attractive for the Late Roman Army was that they were easier to make (experiment shows one can be made in under one hour – Sim 1993), less cumbersome to carry, but arguably just as effective a shock weapon as the *pilum*.

The *pilum* began as a shield-piercing heavy javelin and that was always its main role. The fact that Roman improvements to the weapon or weapons they originally adopted meant it could also be used as a thrusting spear were fortuitous, but never came to supplant that original function. From the 3rd century BC to the 6th century AD, there was always a need for a javelin with a long shank and small head that could punch through a shield and continue in its trajectory in order to wound its target. It was even more attractive because of its useful characteristics of being hard to extract from a shield and so rendering it an encumbrance best discarded. If the *pilum* missed its target and bent on impact, it could not easily be thrown back by the enemy, although it was a simple enough matter to put

An unprovenanced *plumbata* (L: *c.*160mm). (Photo: R. Vermaat)

0

10cm

73

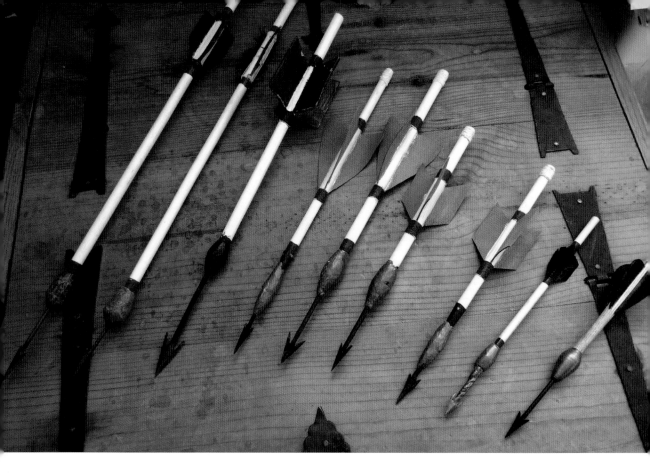

Some reconstructed *plumbatae*.
(Photo: R. Vermaat)

it back into working order after a battle. As such, it had many characteristics in its favour.

It only remains to wonder whether the irony of a modern stand-off glide bomb manufactured by Diehl being named the *Pilum* might have amused a legionary soldier as he cast his *pilum* the short distance between him and his approaching enemy.

SURVIVORS

There are many ferrous components of *pila* to be found in the museums of the Roman world, but no complete example of iron shank and wooden shaft survives. The two bent 1st-century AD *pilum* shanks from Hod Hill, complete with their pyramidal heads, can be found in the Roman Britain gallery of the British Museum in London, while the National Roman Legion Museum in Caerleon has some of the 3rd-century heads from the Prysg Field on display, together with the shank found with them. The Bar Hill *pilum* heads from the 2nd century AD are in the Hunterian Museum in Glasgow University (Scotland), while the near-contemporaneous Croy Hill relief showing the three *pilum*-armed legionaries can be examined in the National Museum of Scotland in Edinburgh. In Germany, *pila* from the early imperial bases along the Lippe are displayed in the Westfälische Römermuseum at Haltern, while fittings (notably the collets) from *pila* lost during the Varus disaster can

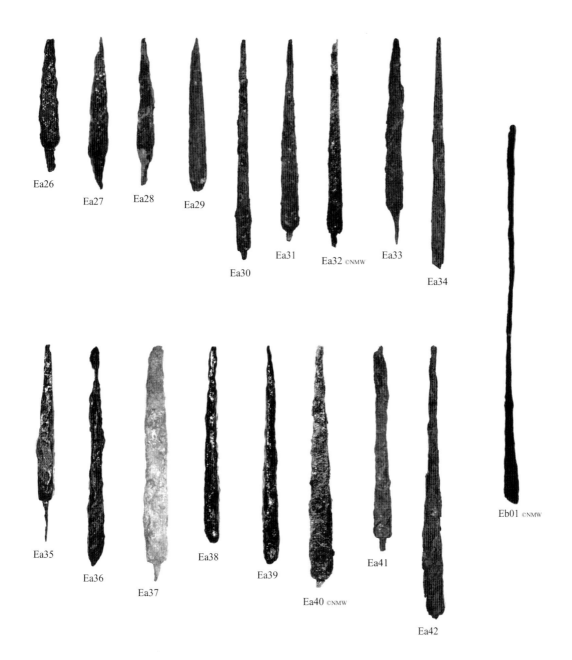

Ea26
Ea27
Ea28
Ea29
Ea30
Ea31
Ea32 ©NMW
Ea33
Ea34
Ea35
Ea36
Ea37
Ea38
Ea39
Ea40 ©NMW
Ea41
Ea42
Eb01 ©NMW

be seen in the Varusschlacht Museum and Park at Kalkriese. *Pila* from the 3rd century AD from Saalburg are on display in the museum in the reconstructed granaries of that fort.

Pilum heads (Ea26–42) and a shank (Eb01) from the Prysg Field, Caerleon. (© National Museum of Wales, photo: E. Chapman)

GLOSSARY

amentum	a **throwing strap**, used to impart greater force or range into casting a javelin.
armatura	Roman weapons drill.
blueing	the process of applying a coat of magnetite to a ferrous object by slowly heating and then **quenching** it.
bodkin	pyramidal tip of a missile, designed to pierce armour (usually square in section).
butt	the rear or lower end of the **shaft**, usually finished with a conical ferrous **ferrule**.
collet	a **ferrule** designed to hold the **iron** and **shaft** together and prevent the **shaft** from splitting at the top.
expansion	broader part of the wooden **shaft** of a *pilum* designed to receive the **tang**.
ferrule	a sleeve or cap that is fitted to a wooden **shaft** to protect it, such as the **collet** or the conical fitting covering the **butt**.
gearing effect	phenomenon whereby a small change to one part of a design often leads to proportionally larger changes elsewhere to compensate for it.
hand grip	that part of the **shaft** designed to be held.
head	tip of the **iron**.
iron	the complete ferrous component, comprising **head**, **shank** and **tang** (or **socket**).
malleolus	hollow missile head used to contain flammable material, normally found on arrows or catapult bolts.
quenching	immersing a ferrous object in liquid after forging, while still hot, in order to harden it by rapid cooling.
Rft	Roman foot (*pes*), *c.*296mm.
Rin	Roman inch (*uncia*), *c.*24mm.
rivet	a pin or nail (sometimes passed through a **rove**) that held the tang within – or fixed the socket to the top – of the **shaft**.
rove	square ferrous plate through which a **rivet** was fastened to the **shaft** to avoid splitting the wood.
shaft	the wooden part of the *pilum* to which the **shank** was attached.
shank	the ferrous neck of the *pilum* **iron**, with the **head** at the top end and the **tang** or **socket** at the bottom (can be circular or square in section, or even both).
socket	hollow end of a **shank**, one of the two principal means of attaching the **shank** to the **shaft**.
tang	that part of the **iron** inserted into the **shaft** to secure it, often with the aid of a **collet**. Can be a spike with one **rivet** or none, or flat, with two or three **rivets**.
throwing strap	see **amentum**.
wedge	small rectangular iron component used to fasten the **collet** to the **shaft**.
weight	spherical attachment located below the **expansion**, possibly made of lead, used to give the *pilum* additional energy.

BIBLIOGRAPHY

Ancient sources

Agathias, *The Histories*.

Ammianus Marcellinus, *The History*. 1939–50 Loeb ed., trans. J.C. Rolfe. Available at http://bit.ly/2cdkW4C

Appian, *Civil Wars*. 1913 Loeb ed., trans. H. White. Available at http://bit.ly/1Q148qp

Appian, *Gallic History*. 1899 Macmillan ed., trans. H. White. Available at http://bit.ly/2cdknI8

Appian, *Hannibal*. 1899 Macmillan ed., trans. H. White. Available at http://bit.ly/2clLnT3

Arrian, *Ektaxis kata Alanoon*. Trans. S. van Dorst. Available at http://bit.ly/2cdl6ZX

Athenaeus, *Deipnosophistae*. 1854 ed., trans. C.D. Yonge. Available at http://bit.ly/2ekKgTL

Aulus Gellius, *Attic Nights*. 1927 Loeb ed., trans. R.C. Rolfe. Available at http://bit.ly/2cdkQdu

[Caesar], *African War*. 1955 Loeb ed., trans. A.G. Wray. Available at http://bit.ly/2dvTGym

Caesar, *Civil War*. 1914 Loeb ed., trans. A.G. Peskett. Available at http://bit.ly/1Srt7YB

Caesar, *Gallic War*. 1917 Loeb ed., trans. H.J. Edwards. Available at http://bit.ly/1VxunsD

Digest. 1932 Central Trust Company ed., trans. S.P. Scott. Available at http://bit.ly/2clMu5l

Dionysius of Halicarnassus, *Roman Antiquities*. 1937–1950 Loeb, trans. E. Cary. Available at http://bit.ly/1NHJ5Y2

Ennius, *Annals*. 1935 Loeb ed., trans. E.H. Warmington. Available at http://bit.ly/2clMi64

Frontinus, *Strategems*. 1925 Loeb ed., trans. C.E. Bennett. Available at http://bit.ly/2clMq5E

Historia Augusta (including the Lives of Hadrian, Severus, Niger, Albinus, Diadumenianus and Aurelian), 1921–32 Loeb, trans. D. Magie. Available at http://bit.ly/2cl9Tnq

Livy, *History of Rome*. 1912, trans. Revd Canon Roberts. Available at http://go.mu.edu/1P3xpRk

Plautus, *Curculio*. 1912 Bell ed., trans. H.T. Riley. Available at http://bit.ly/2cdmMm9

Plautus, *Mostellaria*. Available at http://bit.ly/2clNkPs

Pliny the Elder, *Natural History*. 1855 Taylor & Francis ed., trans. J. Bostock & H.T. Riley. Available at http://bit.ly/2clOASB

Plutarch, *Parallel Lives* (including *Aemilius Paullus*, *Antony*, *Caesar*, *Marius*, *Pompey*, *Romulus*, *Pyrrhus* and *Sulla*). 1923 Loeb ed., trans. B. Perrin. Available at http://bit.ly/2clOHgU

Polybius, *Histories*. 1922–27 Loeb, trans. W.R. Paton. Available at http://bit.ly/1VumvrF

Posidonius, *The Histories*. Available at http://bit.ly/2cdpdoP

Propertius, *Elegies*. Available at http://bit.ly/2cniS7C

Seneca, *On Anger*. 1900 Boehn, trans. A. Stewart. Available at http://bit.ly/2cl9qS9

Servius, *Commentary on the Aeneid of Vergil*. 1881 Teubner ed., Latin text available at http://bit.ly/2en4Oek

Silius Italicus, *Punica*. 1927 Loeb ed., trans. J.D. Duff. Available at http://bit.ly/2cngwpf

Strabo, *The Geography*. 1917–32 Loeb ed., trans. H.L. Jones. Available at http://bit.ly/2cngE8h

Suda. Available online at http://bit.ly/2dwGhpP (N.B. search for 'pilum'.)

Tacitus, *Agricola*. 1876, trans. A.J. Church & W.J. Brodribb. Available at http://bit.ly/1P3xvsb

Tacitus, *Annals* and *Histories*. 1925–37 Loeb, trans. J. Jackson. Available at http://bit.ly/1QyueUm

Varro, *On the Latin Language*. 1938 Loeb, trans. R.G. Kent. Available at http://bit.ly/2ccGy14

Vegetius, *De Re Militari*. 1885 Lang. Available at http://bit.ly/1Qyuz9H

Modern sources

Akerman, J.Y. (1855). 'Note on the angon of Agathias', *Archaeologia* 36: 78–9.

Alapont Martín, L., Calvo Gálvez, M. & Ribera i Lacomba, A. (2010). 'La destrucción de Valencia por Pompeyo (75 a.C.)', *Quaderns de difusió arqueològica* 6: 1–39.

Albrecht, C. (1942). *Das Römerlager in Oberaden und das Uferkastell in Beckinghausen an der Lippe.* 2.2. Dortmund: Veröffentlichung des Städtischen Museums für Vor- und Frühgeschichte Dortmund.

Álvarez Arza, R. & Cubero Argente, M. (1999). 'Los pila del poblado ibérico de Castellruf', *Gladius* 19: 121–42.

Armstrong, J. (2016). *War and Society in Early Rome. From Warlords to Generals.* Cambridge: Cambridge University Press.

Beeser, J. (1979). 'Pilum murale?', *Fundberichte aus Baden-Württemberg* 4: 133–42.

Bennett, J. (1982). 'The Great Chesters "pilum murale"', *Archaeologia Aeliana* ser. 5 X: 200–04.

Bishop, M.C. (1999). 'Praesidium: social, military, and logistical aspects of the Roman army's provincial distribution during the early principate', in A. Goldsworthy & I. Haynes, eds, *The Roman Army as a Community*, JRA Supplementary Series 34, Portsmouth RI: JRA: 111–18.

Bishop, M.C. & Coulston, J.C.N. (2006). *Roman Military Equipment from the Punic Wars to the Fall of Rome.* Oxford: Oxbow Books.

Bongartz, A. (2015). 'Pilum', in Y. Le Bohec, ed., *The Encyclopedia of the Roman Army.* Chichester: Wiley Blackwell, pp. 746–50.

Bonnamour, L. (1990). *Du silex à la poudre: 4000 ans d'armement en val de Saône: exposition, 1990–1991.* Montagnac: Mergoil.

Carney, T.F. (1958). 'Pila at the Battle of Pharsalia', *The Classical Review* 8 (1): 11–13.

Connolly, P. (1997). '*Pilum, gladius* and *pugio* in the Late Republic', *Journal of Roman Military Equipment Studies* 8: 41–57.

Connolly, P. (2000). 'The reconstruction and use of Roman weaponry in the second century BC', *Journal of Roman Military Equipment Studies* 11: 43–6.

Connolly, P. (2001/02). 'The *pilum* from Marius to Nero, a reconsideration of its development and function', *Journal of Roman Military Equipment Studies* 12/13: 1–8.

Cowan, R. (2012). 'The Samnite *pilum*: evidence for Roman boasts', *Ancient Warfare* 6:4: 39–41.

Dahm, O. (1895). 'Das Pilum,' *Bonner Jahrbücher* 96: 226–48.

Feugère, M. (1990). 'Les armes romaines', in L. Bonnamour, ed., *Du silex à la poudre , 4000 ans d'armement en val de Saône*, Montagnac: Mergoil, pp. 93–115.

Geyer, C. (1998). '*Pila in hostes immittunt*', *Journal of Roman Military Equipment Studies* 9: 53–64.

Grab, M. (2011). 'Das marianische Pilum. Der "römische Mythos" im Test', in C. Koepfer, F.W. Himmler & J. Löffl, eds, *Die römische Armee im Experiment*, Berlin: Frank & Timme, pp. 83–92.

Himes, J.B. (2009). *The Old English Epic of Waldere.* Newcastle upon Tyne: Cambridge Scholars Publishing.

Horvat, J. (2002). 'The hoard of Roman Republican weapons from Grad near Šmihel', *Arheološki vestnik* 53, 117–92. Available at http://bit.ly/2a0deYC

Junkelmann, M. (1986). *Die Legionen des Augustus: der römische Soldat im archäologischen Experiment.* Mainz: von Zabern.

Kmetič, D., Horvat, J. & Vodopivec, F. (2004). 'Metallographic examinations of the Roman Republican weapons from the hoard from Grad near Šmihel', *Arheološki vestnik* 55: 291–312.

Köchly, H. (1863). 'Das römische Pilum', in *Vorträge in der 21. und 24. Versammlung der Philologen 1862 in Augsburg*: 139–52.

Lejars, T. (2008). 'Les guerriers et l'armement celto-italique de la nécropole de Monte Bibele', in D. Vitali & S. Verger, eds, *Tra mondo celtico e mondo italico: la necropoli di Monte Bibele: atti della tavola rotonda.* Bologna: Università di Bologna, pp. 127–222.

Lindenschmit, L. (1881). 'Das schwere Pilum', in L. Lindenschmit, ed., *Alterthümer unserer heidnischen Vorzeit* Bd.2, Mainz: Taf. 7, pp. 1–11.

Lindenschmit, L. (1882). *Tracht und Bewaffnung des römischen Heeres während der Kaiserzeit*. Braunschweig: Vieweg & Sohn.

Luik, M. (2000). 'Republikanische Pilumfunde vom "Talamonaccio"/Italien', *Archaeologisches Korrespondenzblatt* 30: 269–77.

Luik, M. (2002): *Die Funde aus den römischen Lagern um Numantia im Römisch-Germanischen Zentralmuseum*, Kataloge vor- und frühgeschichtlicher Altertümer 31, Mainz: RGZM.

McDonnell-Staff, P. (2011). 'The peg that would break: Marius and the *pilum*, a Roman myth', *Ancient Warfare* 5.1: 34–6.

Matthew, C. (2010). 'The Battle of Vercellae and the alteration of the heavy javelin (*pilum*) by Gaius Marius – 101 BC', *Antichthon* 44: 50–67.

Quesada Sanz, F. (1997). *El armamento ibérico. Estudio tipológico, geográfico, funcional, social y simbólico de las armas en la Cultura Ibérica (siglos VI–I a. C.)*, 2 vols. Monographies Instrumentum, 3. Montagnac: Ed. Monique Mergoil.

Quesada Sanz, F. (2007). 'Hispania y el ejército romano republicano. Interaccón y adopción de tipos metálicos/Hispania and the Republican Roman Army. Interaction and adoption of weapon types', in C. Fernández, ed., *Metalistería de la Hispania Romana*. Número monográfico de Sautuola 13, pp. 379–401.

Reinach, A.-J. (1877–1917), 'Pilum', in C.V. Daremberg & E. Saglio, eds, *Dictionnaire des antiquités grecques et romaines, d'après les textes et les monuments*. Paris: Hachette, pp. 481–84.

Reinach, A.-J. (1907), 'L'origine du pilum', *Revue Archéologique* 10: 226–44.

Schnurbein, S. von (1974), 'Zum Ango', in G. Kossack & G. Ulbert, eds, *Studien zur vor- und frühgeschichtlichen Archäologie. Festschrift für Joachim Werner z. 65. Geburtstag*, Munich: Beck, pp. 411–33.

Schulten, A. (1911), 'Der Ursprung des Pilums', *Rheinisches Museum für Philologie* 66: 573–84.

Schulten, A. (1960), 'Pilum', *Paulys Realencyclopädie der classischen Altertumswissenschaft* 20.2: 1333–69.

Sim, D. (1992), 'The manufacture of disposable weapons for the Roman army', *Journal of Roman Military Equipment Studies* 3: 105–19.

Underwood, R. (1999). *Anglo-Saxon Weapons and Warfare*. Stroud: Tempus.

Vicente, J.D., Pilar Punter, M. & Ezquerra, B. (1997). 'La catapulta tardo-republicana y otro equipamiento militar de "La Caridad" (Caminreal, Teruel)', *JRMES* 8: 167–99.

Willaume, M. (1987). 'Les objets de la vie quotidienne', in *Archéologie d'Entremont au Musée Granet, Aix-en-Provence 1987*: 107–42.

Wylie, W.M. (1870), 'Observations on the Roman pilum', *Archaeologia* 42: 327–46.

Zhmodikov, A. (2000). 'Roman Republican heavy infantrymen in battle (IV–II centuries B.C.)', *Historia* 49(1): 67–78.

Adamclisi metopes 27 and 28 depicting legionaries with shouldered *pila* held below the centre of gravity. (Photo: C. Chirita)

INDEX